Dominic Rowsell

"Ian and Dominic's sharp and lucid analysis of what works and what doesn't is both compelling and instructive. This is a must read for any business in a competitive market place."
René Carayol, author, internationally renowned business guru, and media personality

"I really enjoyed reading the book. In fact, once I started I wanted to finish reading to the end in one sitting. Why? Well, the book has some really solid messages and has a good way of putting it over. I feel I need to read again and plan to dip back when I need a refresh. It is easy and amusing and so should probably be read once and then referred to again and again."
Mark Varney, Strategic Sales Director, Atos Origin

"Coming from the procurement field I was pleasantly surprised to find how readable the book is even though I am not well acquainted with all the associated jargon. I was much impressed by the comprehensive action plans and by the substantiation of the effectiveness of these provided by the customer endorsements – the proof of the pudding is in the eating!

My only regret is that the book was not written 25 years ago as it would have enabled me to better understand where sales and marketing people were coming from because where they wish to go they always make abundantly clear."
Stephen Wicks, Head of Procurement, European Space Agency

"Direct, pungent and straight to the point A book that finally takes marketing out of the box and onto the next level. Why Killer Products annihilates all conventional thinking on the subject and offers a radical new recipe for dealing with customers. Consolidated mental processes are reprogrammed in order to be capable of perceiving needs in a new way and create a durable linkage with the Customer. The result is an infallible marketing strategy which generates and sustains added value over time. In essence the book

provides an innovative set of tools capable of dealing with today's marketing chaos, and this I must say is no simple matter. Well done."

Nigel Zanenga, Global Network Manager East Asia, UniCredit

"Strategy is good, execution is even better, but nothing else counts if sales are on the floor. Ian and Dominic have written a lucid and energetic book that gets to the bottom of the fundamental sales problem: killer (and other) products rarely walk straight out of the door. The key contribution is simple, like the best ideas – sales fail if we miss the value culture dominating the thoughts and actions of buyers. It's not a difficult door to unlock because this actionable book provides the keys. Highly recommended to thoughtful leaders."

Jyoti Banerjee, Co-founder, M Institute

A sale is the key and core element of every successful business. There are a 1000+ books available around the subject. But Why Killer Products Don't Sell is different as it uses a very strong angle which is buying behaviour. Whether you are a service company or a product focused organization, no company continues to have a killer product as markets evolve. Therefore even the best products need a competitive sales approach. This book gives you very good insight and ideas on how to optimise your sales process. The examples can easily be related your own situations and is recommended to anyone who wants to grow their business.

Steen Foldberg, Managing Director, Merrill Lynch Luxembourg

WHY KILLER PRODUCTS DON'T SELL

WHY KILLER PRODUCTS DON'T SELL

How to run your company to a new set of rules

Ian Gotts &
Dominic Rowsell

CAPSTONE

Other Wiley Editorial Offices

John Wiley & Sons Inc., 111 River Street, Hoboken, NJ 07030, USA

Jossey-Bass, 989 Market Street, San Francisco, CA 94103-1741, USA

Wiley-VCH Verlag GmbH, Boschstr. 12, D-69469 Weinheim, Germany

John Wiley & Sons Australia Ltd, 42 McDougall Street, Milton, Queensland 4064, Australia

John Wiley & Sons (Asia) Pte Ltd, 2 Clementi Loop #02-01, Jin Xing Distripark,
     Singapore 129809

John Wiley & Sons Canada Ltd, 6045 Freemont Blvd., Mississauga, Ontario, Canada
     L5R 4J3

Wiley also publishes its books in a variety of electronic formats. Some content that
appears in print may not be available in electronic books.

A catalogue record for this book is available from the British Library and the Library of
Congress.

ISBN 978-1-90-646-526-1 (H/B)

Typeset by Macmillan Publishing Solutions, India
Printed and bound in Great Britain by CPI Antony Rowe, Chippenham, Wiltshire
Illustrations by Stuart Roper, stuart@milagrodesign.co.uk

Substantial discounts on bulk quantities of Capstone Books are available to corporations,
professional associations and other organizations. For details telephone John Wiley & Sons
on (+44) 1243-770441, fax (+44) 1243 770571 or email corporatedevelopment@wiley.com

Contents

Acknowledgments

Some say that experience is standing on the shoulders of giants. In this case it is climbing over the piles of obsolete stock and failed products. We could only write this book because many, many people in the corporate world were prepared to open up old wounds and relive the pain and anguish of seeing their potential world-breaking product end up on the junk heap. And then picking themselves up, learning from it, and trying again. And again. And again.

As you can see from the list below, these are not dotcom boom and bust companies. They range from the highly respected Fortune 1000 companies through successful mid-market businesses to the rising stars of tomorrow.

EADS: www.eads.com; 113,000 employees; Jeremy Greaves – Vice President Communications & PR, UK

Cisco Systems: www.cisco.com; 64,000 employees; Nick Watson – VP, Europe

Fuji Xerox Global Services: www.fujixerox.com; 40,000 employees; Andy Berry – General Manager

Symantec: www.symantec.com; 17,500 employees; Martin Brown – Senior Sales Director

SAS: www.sas.com; 10,500 employees; Robert Mercer – Regional Director

Nimbus: www.nimbuspartners.com; 130 employees; Adrian King – Chief Operating Officer

Fourth Hospitality: www.fourthhospitality.com; 100 employees; Ben Hood – Managing Director

First Recovery: www.firstrecovery.co.uk; 50 employees; Paul Jackson – Managing Director

81G: www.81G.org; 30 employees; Samantha Hinton – joint Managing Director

DanielsReeve: www.danielsreeve.com; 7 employees; Nick Daniels – Managing Director

And finally our thanks go to the team at Wiley and to those closest to us, who have given us the space and time to write another book, especially Anna who painstakingly transcribed hours of interview recordings and Natalie who patiently applied her Classics degree to my grammar.

Sensibilities and Political Correctness: For the benefit of simplicity throughout this book, 'salesman' means saleswoman, salesperson, sales rep, account manager, and customer business developer. We recognize that some (most?) of the most successful sales people today are women. When we say 'he' we mean 'he/she/it'.

Foreword

There is nothing more soul destroying for an evangelist, an investor, and most of all, for a founder than a truly innovative product which never fulfils its revenue promise. A little bit of you dies as every week the sales quotas are not met until the product is relegated to the dumpster.

I love starting companies, investing in start-ups, and promoting great products. But what I *really* love is seeing them succeed. And success is measured in dollars, so selling is job number 1, number 2 and number 3. *Crossing the Chasm* by Geoffrey Moore clearly showed that there are different buyers with very different buying habits. But, despite these insights, little has been written to help entrepreneurs (and intrapreneurs) understand how to transform their brilliant ideas into products or services that companies want to buy and are able to buy.

What is missing is an understanding from the buyer's perspective on what they go through when they make decisions about buying innovative and disruptive technology. Only then can the entrepreneurs understand how to align themselves and support their buyer. So this book is about sales, but not about sales technique or a detailed sales methodology. This is far more fundamental than that. This turns most hardened sales professional's ideas and prejudices about sales on their head, and buries them forever.

This book provides practical and implementable actions that you can apply to your organization, tomorrow. It is designed to "make a difference" whether you are leading a start-up, innovating inside a corporation, or standing on the sidelines as an investor cheering the team on. I wish more entrepreneurs like Ian and Dominic would make time to capture their valuable experience of building successful companies. If we did, then probably fewer ground breaking products and services would wither on the vine starved of that critical life-giving resource; sales revenue. Let's drink to that.

Guy Kawasaki, 2008

Guy Kawasaki is a founding partner and entrepreneur-in-residence at Garage Technology Ventures. He is also the co-founder of Alltop.com, an "online magazine rack" of popular topics on the web. Previously, he was an Apple Fellow at Apple Computer, Inc. Guy is the author of eight books including *The Art of the Start, Rules for Revolutionaries, How to Drive Your Competition Crazy, Selling the Dream*, and *The Macintosh Way*. He has a BA from Stanford University and an MBA from UCLA as well as an honorary doctorate from Babson College.

Introduction

WHAT THIS BOOK IS ABOUT

You all thought it was a killer product, but sales flopped

You're a major corporation with a track record of strong sales for your current product range. You've worked long and hard to produce a unique innovative product that you know the market needs. It should have flown out of the warehouse, but sales tanked and it has hit the morale and commissions of the sales team. Why?

Alternatively, you are a nimble start-up with experienced founders, who have built their reputation on sales in previous large corporations. Again, you've developed a ground-breaking product and made some early sales. To really ramp up revenues you have decided to sell through the channel, or you've hired a hotshot salesman. But nothing is happening. The only sales are being made by the founders. Why?

There is more than one type of sales

It has long been understood that different sales techniques are required depending on the type and maturity of the product, the industry, size of customer, and the market. Some people think 'sales is sales is sales', and that any good salesman can simply change or morph their technique to suit the particular circumstance. But over 15 years of research into business-to-business sales has shown that this thinking is fatally flawed. There are sales techniques, but these are fine-tuning. What really make the difference are four clearly defined 'buying cultures'.

The maturity of the product in the customer's mind determines which of the four buying cultures is appropriate, and this is most stark in the purchase of technology or software. So, it is not surprising that there is a startling parallel between the buying cultures and the Technology Adoption Life Cycle principles that Geoffrey Moore made popular in his books *Crossing the Chasm* and *Inside the Tornado*[1], which focus on buying technology.

This book will help you:

- Understand why killer products don't sell.
- Appreciate that there are four *very* different ways of selling, based on the customer's buying culture.
- Appreciate that sales today require you to sell to a buyer in such a way that he wants to buy.
- Realize that how you create value is a *very* different proposition from the traditional 'sales is sales is sales' approach.
- Understand how to engage your entire organization to support Value Created sales.
- Find a methodology to transform your organization to be *much* more successful.

So, if you have a killer product, here's how to ensure it really does sell . . .

WHY WE WROTE THIS BOOK

Crossing the Chasm and *Inside the Tornado*, by Geoffrey Moore, are essential reading for every marketer in the technology field. In his books, Moore describes beautifully the dynamics of a disruptive marketplace, and the fundamental customer traits at different stages of market maturity. But there was not space within those books to give any insights on

---

[1] *Crossing the Chasm* and *Inside the Tornado* by Geoffrey Moore. A summary of both books is given in the Appendix.

how a company should organize itself, and operate based on the needs of different buyers. As profound (yet obvious) as *Crossing the Chasm* is in assessing the customer's perspective, there is something equally profound (and obvious) to be said about the supplier's perspective. Each different customer type needs a radically different method of engagement.

So, we wrote this book because we have seen products fail in company after company. Yet we've seen far less compelling products soar once the organizations have understood the four *buying cultures* (see page 12), the corresponding *operational cultures* (see page 13), and the *IMPACT buying cycle* (see page 21).

There are only so many companies that we can educate, work with, and support at any one time.[2] This book needed to be written to enable us to help more companies understand how to get their innovative products to market. Nothing in the book is pure theory. Nothing is conjecture. Nothing is unproven. Some of the case studies are from global corporates, making an impact on the world with their innovative products. Others are small start-ups, embarking on their own quiet revolution.

We hope that you will gain as much from reading this book as we did from researching and writing it.

A BAR IN ROTTERDAM

This story started in a bar in Rotterdam in 1992. I was consulting to a Dutch oil exploration company because at that time the oil industry was going through one of its transitions, and the old-style 'roughneck' manager needed to become more of a leader in the field. At the end of a

---

[2] The ultimate disruptive technology – cloning – does not seem to have made it to the market yet, so there are only two of us.

particularly long day I was having a beer with their Managing Director (MD); we got onto the subject of suppliers and their ability to align to the complex business needs of an exploration rig. The MD was not happy with his suppliers, from the caterers to the mud technologists. He saw them as one of the factors holding back the cultural evolution of his business. He knew that there were some suppliers who could contribute much more than they did, and there were others who tried to do too much. At one end of the spectrum they needed too much management attention, and at the other end his managers were developing ideas that suppliers had already perfected. I asked him to describe to me what a perfect supplier engagement would look like. It was not so much what he said which sparked my imagination, but what he did *not* say and the great difficulty he had in not saying it. I took his description of a supplier engagement and laid it out as a process, and by doing this I realized his problem. He was not articulating a single supplier engagement but *multiple* engagements, and the factors which changed the engagements were not just what the supplier was offering but *what that offering meant to him* at that particular moment in time.

What followed were several years of listening, observing, and learning from other people's successes and failures, and bit by bit I was able to show how all these successes and failures followed a common pattern. I got the answer to my original question, and the realization that there was a huge gap in accepted practices in sales. One other major realization was that selling is one of the greatest global employers – it is a social science, and as such should be a serious degree subject, but it is not. No serious university on the planet offers sales as a degree subject, and that is something we would like to see change.

In summary: You can win *much* more business and your products will sell *much* more effectively if you understand a Value Created sale. This book explains what you need to know. So, what started in a bar in Rotterdam has turned into a global consulting business and now a book – and possibly a degree subject . . .

WHO SHOULD READ THIS BOOK

This book is intended to be a catalyst for action aimed at a range of people inside and outside your organization. Here are just a few, and why it is relevant to them:

Chief Executive Officer

As CEO you are responsible for the overall performance of the business. That means the critical decision about which business model or models to apply should rest with you – or at least with you and your executive team. You determine how innovative you want the company to be, and the associated investment that goes with it. You need to see a return on that investment. You need ways to measure and evaluate your R&D, which is normally characterized as black-ops or special projects; or art rather than science.

This book will give you the framework to make these decisions, resulting in science rather than the art of the possible.

Chief Executive Officer of a start-up

If you are leading a start-up, unless you have decided to take on an existing player with your me-too product, you probably have an innovative, paradigm-shifting, trend-leaping product. The unfortunate thing is that you have probably already hired a hotshot, big-ticket salesman, who has been successful with a 'generate lead – handle objections – close deal' approach. You know, as founders, in your heart of hearts, that this approach won't work, but you need to scale. The only savior is the market. If your market matures really quickly, you may suddenly find yourself in a competitive market. Then you probably have the right sales team and business model. But if you are not the gorilla[3] in the market, you may have a torrid time competing against the market leader. Then the only place of safety is in a niche that you can protect well.

[3] Gorilla – a marketing term for the dominant player in the market, the market leader.

This book will show you how to align your approach to the market, rather than waiting for the market to align with you.

Chief Operations Officer

You are responsible for optimizing the operation of the entire business; for ensuring that each of the moving parts delivers a seamless experience for the customer and a great working environment for the employee. You know that sales are made by more than just the sales teams. You also get frustrated by the R&D spend which gets wasted when the products fail to sell. What if you could improve the success rate – dramatically? Running a company with sales going through the roof and money pouring in is easier than launching the latest cost-cutting initiative or turning down the funding for a new product idea.[4]

This book will help you understand how you organize the entire company, not just sales, to sell innovative products.

Sales Director

The challenge you face depends on the size of your organization, the span of products, and your background. If you are Sales Director of a major multinational, you will have a wide range of products. Some will have been developed in-house and others from acquisitions. They will vary in market maturity. Understanding the best approach for selling each of these products is critical if they are all to succeed. Simply creating one sales team and putting all the products on the price list will not work – appealing though it sounds. A single product start-up is simpler, but the challenges remain the same.

A sound understanding of the principles in this book will help you recruit, organize, measure, lead, and coach your sales teams.

---

[4] Just ask the guys at Google.

Head of M&A

Your job is to buy companies for the organization and then sell off the bits that don't fit with the overall corporate strategy. But now you have another consideration when you buy that new innovative start-up with a really sexy new product. Is the company geared up to sell an innovative product? Or is it just going to add the new product to the existing salesmen's price list? Or worse, chuck it onto the company's e-commerce site? The implication is that a consideration of the sales approach should at least influence the M&A strategy for the company – what products to sell off, which to support, and which ones to buy. You can also acquire products that are underperforming in other companies confident that you can make them fly off the shelves in your company.

Using the ideas in this book, you can formulate your M&A strategy.

CMO/Head of Marketing

Are you viewed as the team that develops brochures and sources leads for the latest whizzy product, or are you part of an integrated and innovative sales machine? How do you know what marketing spend will contribute most? It's easy to spend time and money that goes nowhere. And with innovative products, you have relatively little time to get it right.

The ideas in this book will help you decide on your marketing strategy, and understand when and how marketing should lead sales. You'll find this book is the perfect companion to *Crossing the Chasm* and *Inside the Tornado*, as it explains how you work with the rest of the company.

Investors and VCs

Before you invest in a company, does it have the correct business model? It's a pretty fundamental question. But simply asking the management of the company is probably not enough. They are hardly going to admit that they don't. So how are you going to validate that they are on track?

Clearly this is not the only due diligence you'll do. You still need to evaluate the management team, the product, the market, and the competition. Now, using the approach in this book, you have another lens or perspective which will make you ask some different questions throughout the due diligence. Take a look at your existing portfolio. How many companies with great products are failing to meet the expectations they had when you invested? Have you and your management simply written them off; you get some stars and some dogs. You make so much on the stars that the dogs don't matter to the portfolio. What if that didn't have to be true? What if you could help the dogs become stars? This book will help you understand how to de-risk your investments.

Head of Innovation

Your title gives the game away. You are there to be innovative. And if the company can afford to have a Head of Innovation, it's probably a relatively large and mature business.[5] You will have a portfolio of products and your role is to bring in new innovative products. So, where are the innovative products going to come from?

If your role is to look for innovative products in the market and acquire them, then you should look back at the Head of M&A/Investors and VCs sections. If your role is to generate innovative ideas internally across the whole company – or just within your team – then a fundamental question is, "How will the new sexy, innovative product be taken to market?" Will it be through the existing sales teams? This book will enable you to answer that fundamental question, based on theory backed up with experience.

---

[5] If it isn't – it's a pretentious over capitalized start-up.

HOW TO USE THIS BOOK

This book is intended to be the catalyst for action. We hope that the ideas and examples inspire you to act. So, do whatever you need to do to make this book useful. Use Post-it notes, photocopy pages, scan pages, and write on it. Go to our website and email colleagues the e-book summary. Lend it. Rip it apart, or read it quickly in one sitting. Whatever works for you.

We hope this becomes your most dog-eared book.

Send us your feedback

We love feedback. We prefer great reviews, but we'll accept anything that helps take the ideas further. The ideas have resulted from every single person we've worked with. We welcome your comments on this book.

We'd prefer email, as it's easy to answer and saves trees. If the ideas worked for you, we'd love to hear your success stories. Maybe we could turn them into video or audio interviews on our website, www.killer-products.com, so others can learn from you. That's one of the reasons why we wrote this book. So talk to us.

ian@killer-products.com

dominic@killer-products.com

feedback@killer-products.com

CHAPTER 1

Some killer products really don't sell

SO MANY PRODUCTS, SO FEW SALES

There are great products in the marketplace, but great products don't automatically mean overnight success – or even long-term success. In many cases, really innovative products not only fail to capture the market, but are swamped by inferior competition. Stories of entrepreneurial success and failure tend to focus on the product, without looking at the company behind the product: the culture, the business model, the sales approach, the back-office support. But this is where the magic ingredients are mixed into the secret sauce.[6]

Despite highly visible failures, the entrepreneurial spirit is stronger than ever in every corner of the world. This is fuelled partially by the relative ease with which a software product or website offering can be brought to market. And now, software is a critical and compelling part of every piece of hardware.

---

[6] Don't worry – We won't lapse into Harry Potter/Delia Smith similes and analogies. We just got a little carried away.

1

Consider the iPhone – without the beautifully tactile user interface it would just be another elegant (and expensive) piece of jewelry; or your BlackBerry – which needs layer upon layer of technology to push your messages to you wherever you are in the world, and bill you for the pleasure.

The line between a product and a service is becoming blurred in many areas. Therefore, we will use the term 'product' in the book to mean hardware, hardware + software, software installed on a device, Software as a Service (SaaS), or a pure service offering.

With the constant innovation of the software development platforms, it is easier to develop really exciting and compelling user experiences. Added to this, the range of delivery platforms is expanding: from the wacky Microsoft Surface™,[7] through laptops, to smartphones which are permanently connected to the GPS and the Web. And now the iPhone has been opened up as a development platform. We need to be clear that innovative or disruptive products don't exist only in the technology sector, but often a product or a service is made possible by back-office technology.

On television we watch programs like *The Apprentice* or *Dragons' Den*, where eager, passionate, blinded, and desperate entrepreneurs and inventors believe they have created the killer product. The product which will have the world beating a path to their doors. These people are a microcosm of the greater business world, where large and expensive R&D departments go through essentially the same process.

Possibly the greatest output from R&D departments is blind faith. Many R&D teams adopt the attitude of "Don't trouble us with your talk of sales, delivery, or measurement since we are not just inventors – we are artists in our industry."[8]

---

[7] Think 'games computer trapped inside your coffee table'.
[8] Although it is said that true innovation is 1% inspiration and 99% perspiration – which is probably why software engineers and inventors smell so bad.

A small tangent – Blind Faith. This was formed by Steve Winwood and Eric Clapton when they were both at a loose end after the break ups of Traffic and Cream at the end of 1968. Winwood and Clapton got together in early 1969 at Clapton's house to jam, but word got out and Ginger Baker turned up to join in on drums. Ric Grech, from Family, was the last to join, on bass to free up Steve Winwood. I suppose one could say that this super-group had the makings of a killer product? Anyway, Robert Stigwood got them into a studio where they recorded several excellent songs, but the rush to release an album meant that the second side was filled with a long and rather uninteresting jam. They debuted in front of 100,000 people at a free concert in Hyde Park and then set off for a USA tour. Blind Faith fell apart on tour in August 1969 due to the uncritical hero worship and adulation from the American crowds, which offered no challenge for their musicianship, and the lack of opportunity to develop their music privately. Exit one killer product.

Ooga Labs is a very good example of this mass production of new products. Ooga Labs is a technology greenhouse based in downtown San Francisco developing four to six consumer Internet businesses simultaneously. Their purpose is to build unique Internet products to be used by millions, and Ooga has a company culture capable of churning these new products out *ad infinitum*. Ooga Labs is self-funded and thus has total control over the direction of its products. It only develops its own ideas and, of those products which it creates, only the ones that appear to Ooga to have a chance of becoming the next big thing will be fully developed. Ooga relies on finding the best software engineers because at Ooga, 'building stuff' is job number one and so engineering is skill number one. By developing multiple products under one roof, Ooga Labs believes it has the best of a startup, a big company, an R&D lab, a movie studio, and a venture capital firm all under one roof. Ooga has set a goal of eight 'company starts' in four years. Only time and history will tell us if the model works.

These days it is easy to build products, and there are more places where they can be used – which sounds great. But remember, success isn't proportional to the quality or the degree of innovation of the product – and business buyers and consumers are swamped with choice. Paint all this innovation on the canvas of a rapidly evolving marketplace and truly global competition, and the statistical chance of failure is huge.

But that hasn't stopped innovation. More products are being brought to market every year, and probably another 100 will have been launched worldwide before you finish reading this book.[9] That can only spell one thing: 98 of those 100 products launched will be stillborn, with the entre-preneurial flames burning within many talented people being snuffed out, along with their savings or investors' funds.

 Surely there must be a better way? Or maybe this is simply technologi-cal Darwinism in action: adapt to survive, or you will become extinct.

HEROIC FAILURES

History is littered with promising products which faltered badly or ultimately failed in both the business-to-consumer (B2C) world and the business-to-business (B2B) world. The consumer world has the best-known stories, such as VHS vs. Sony's Betamax in the 1980s.

A replay of VHS vs. Betamax was the battle for the next-generation DVD player market which, in the end, was won by Sony with Blu-ray. Toshiba, which was backed by players like Microsoft, had to resort to slashing

---

[9] This is not a comment on your reading speed. I love the comment "I've just come back from France – I've been finishing my latest book. I'm a very slow reader."

the prices of its next-generation HD-DVD players as a last-ditch effort to save the format. But Toshiba did not lose the new DVD format battle in the B2C world. No, in 2007 they had 50 percent of the market. And then Sony outsmarted Toshiba by selling the Blu-ray concept to Warner Brothers, i.e. B2B. As Gartner analyst Paul O'Donovan said, "It shows what a highly competitive market it is. When it comes to video, it's the person with the most content that wins." Warner Brother's decision means that an estimated three-quarters of new film releases will only be available on Blu-ray discs, and that signaled the end of an 18-month campaign and a multimillion-dollar investment by Toshiba.

The B2B market has an equal number of examples of 'nails hit squarely on the thumb'. It's just that they are not dinner party or tabloid newspaper stories. One of the reasons is that there is nothing quite so embarrassing as failed technology,[10] and generally speaking major corporates don't like bad PR. They have developed a habit of allowing small companies to take the risks of innovation and then snapping them up when it looks as if they have traction, or standing well back should they fail. If the failures are internal, then they're buried early in life.

There are many examples. Why did a killer product like IP Telephony take so long to pick up? Why weren't SGI's blisteringly fast servers adopted by data centers? And whatever happened to the Psion Organizer? Why is it not up there with the iPhone and the BlackBerry?

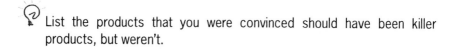 List the products that you were convinced should have been killer products, but weren't.

---

[10] How many of you remember the pride of British automotive technology in 1950, the V16 BRM which failed to leave the starting line at Silverstone? The fans threw pennies onto the track. Ouch!

A very good example of a killer product which did not make it in the B2B world is Radix from TSB International, described by Richard Beasley, now a Sales Director at BT who was tasked with selling it at the time, as follows:

"*TSB International, Canada worked closely with Nortel who had their global HQ in Mississauga, the same town as TSB. The product they had was called Radix, a network management system aimed at the PBX and voice network service providers.*

Radix was well ahead of its time. It was incredibly powerful, with a UNIX operating system and Oracle database. As a result it was highly available, running on IBM RS 6000 and the HP RISC equivalent, and had the scalability to support thousands of end-point devices. The functionality was much more advanced than the off-the-shelf systems like HP Open View and IBM's Tivoli. Until Radix, service companies like BT had to have an army of engineers on site to keep their customers' PBXs running and maintained. Radix meant that for every one hundred PBXs connected via an on-site 'black box', technology that TSB manufactured in house, you needed one less engineer; sixty-five to seventy percent of all faults could be fixed remotely, and automatic inventory control meant that in the event of a hardware failure the correct part could be dispatched to site with the engineer. This had a dramatic impact on improving customer service levels and reducing operating costs of the service provider, and on the face of it the ability to create some compelling business cases. There were even plans to extend its capability into toll fraud, a real problem at the time. In the end, poor marketing and a sales team that really didn't understand how to sell the business benefits sealed its fate. The sales effort was all far too technology-focused, and in the end it became too much hassle to continue its development so we ended up selling the IPR. Eventually TSB International was acquired by Peregrine Systems."

Chris Huggett, Sales VP at 3Com, on a faltered Killer Solution:

"I've seen killer solutions that don't sell. When I was Director of Vertical Marketing at Cisco back in 2001/2, we found that retailers were keen to do in-store advertising. They wanted to give customers an in-store experience of something other than just the price ticket and the packaging. This makes sense to lots of product categories, like oral healthcare, or breakfast cereals. It was quite a sensible attempt to pinch some of the advertising dollars from commercial television. It would mean that brands would be advertising to the consumer at the point where they're making the buying decision. The challenge is getting those moving sexy images and sound to the consumer standing in the aisle. Retailers were mucking about with PC based systems, in-store DVDs etc. and it was all pretty rudimentary.

Anyway, Cisco used its strong brand to pull together the ad agency, WPP, as well as Sony. At the time plasma screen technology was coming down in price, broadband availability was increasing massively and ad agencies were getting their heads around what a message might look like in the five or six second commercial. So, timing was right to go and see the big retailers.

The pitch was compelling "We know you're concerned about this and it's a business issue. We think the technology is now in place for an in-store advertising solution. There are people who can manage the programming channel for you 24 hours a day. You can do all sorts of clever stuff like changing your prices up and down the country in all your stores from head office. Just change the price through your desktop, through all the stores in the country within seconds." That seemed like an absolute killer product. Anyway we invested a lot of money, created a big marketing budget, created a team of people from WPP/Sony/Cisco talking to Marketing Directors and Managing Directors of big retailers.

It failed completely. The account managers were classic sales guys who were prisoners of the CIO. The CIO says "I don't want video on my network. I've got enough trouble already keeping the network stable without adding new applications to it." The account managers were cowed by this. They thought "I can see where my $6 million quota is going to come from with this guy, so I'm not going to antagonize him by going over to the business guys and having a conversation about running video advertising across the network."

The retailer in question (a household name in the UK) ran a pilot in three stores. They ended up buying something that looked a lot like the original plan, two years later but not from Cisco. So, a really smart bunch of people came together, created something, put it on the table – us. Then some tiny company ran off with the spoils. It was a real failure of imagination by the account team, playing the percentages rather than seriously trying to add value to the customer's business."

SO FIRSTLY, WHAT IS A FAILURE?

Failure is not just a discontinued product or a bankrupt company, although these are pretty stark measures of failure. At the other end of the 'failure spectrum' are products which fail to gather the expected market share and never become the dominant gorilla in the marketplace. They could still be profitable. But they are burning up resource which could and should be deployed to more profitable areas. Those products are holed up in a niche market being the best at something very, very specific, failing to fulfill their full potential. Their time is past. But how could it have been? Imagine how David Potter and the guys at Psion must feel looking at the success of the iPhone.

Let's play the blame game. Someone must be to blame for all this waste.

"Shares in Riversoft, the network management software group, plunged almost 25 per cent on Monday morning as the company warned that 'a sudden and severe deterioration' in the completion of orders led to second-quarter sales significantly below expectations.

I have never seen a quarter unravel so quickly. Things went from OK to dire in the space of a week at the end of the quarter. We were at the stage where we had met technical requirements, agreed contracts and drawn up the paperwork only for the deals to be closed down in the finance department."

Phil Tee, Chairman and Chief Technology Officer
Source: FT

News reports like this were quite commonplace in the dotcom bust, but they are far from unknown today. It would be easier and less embarrassing to simply explain away these failures as "too early for the market" or "delivering to a market which evolved too quickly".

There is a saying that "the future is here, it's just unevenly distributed". What that means is, with a global market and the opportunity to market through the Internet to access that global market, you could probably find a group of customers for whom your product is not too early. But, think of this: if you are launching innovative products then you need to be able to market to the Early Adopters who were described in Moore's *Crossing the Chasm*. Therefore, by definition, you need to be world class at educating, shaping, and leading the market.

Alternatively, the blame is laid at the door of sales. The sales teams were inexperienced or were not the A players. Sure they could get the customer interested, but could never close. There are examples where these new innovative products were simply put on the price list so every salesman could sell them. The results have been the same. Nothing.

Perhaps the multimillion marketing budget was not available, a clear-cut argument. But there are examples where the product was beaten by an underfunded product whose marketing budget ran on fresh air.

Anyway, here are some of the more popular types of blame. Pick yours at your leisure:

CDNU – Customers Did Not Understand

WWTE – We Were Too Early

BLUD – Bank Let Us Down

CMIC – Chinese Made It Cheaper

MPUW – Marketing Positioned Us Wrong

MSOI – Megacorp Stole Our Idea

SASS – Salesmen Are So Stupid

There is a common theme across all these acronyms. THE CUSTOMER IS NOT BUYING. Notice, we didn't say the company isn't selling enough of the product – the customer lies at the heart of the problem. So, how should you relate to the very different buyers with their very different ways of purchasing?

CHAPTER 2

It's not how you sell, but how customers buy

SALES IS SALES IS SALES – RIGHT?

Why is it that organizations appear to behave in totally different ways when it comes to making decisions such as buying something? What is it that is driving and controlling what can sometimes appear to be erratic and illogical behavior?

It has long been believed that any one of the different sales methodologies will help you sell, irrespective of the type of product, the industry, the size of customer, or the market. It's viewed that 'sales is sales is sales', and that any good salesman can simply change or morph their approach to suit the particular circumstance. There are no shortage of selling methodologies, such as Strategic Selling, TAS, Powerbase Selling, Solution Selling, Value Selling, The Complex Sale, Impax, and SPIN, to name a few.

Our 15 years of research and consulting on sales has spanned the range of organizations – from the largest global corporates turning over

$100 billion down to small companies with two employees who are just starting out. The research has revealed some remarkable results: the accepted thinking on sales methodologies is fundamentally flawed. The methodologies will help fine-tune your sales team and increase their productivity, but they will not determine whether your killer product will find its way to the customers.

When did you last question the fundamentals of your sales process, rather than your salesmen?

It's your ability to engage with the customer's very clearly defined buying culture which will make the differences. And the buying culture is determined by product maturity. There are four buying cultures, which are distinct, and each requires a different engagement approach. These buying cultures, not surprisingly, show some degree of congruence with the different buyers described in *Crossing the Chasm* and *Inside the Tornado*.

It may be hard to believe that corporates like Cisco struggle to sell innovative products. Surely they have the brand, marketing muscle, and distribution channel to be able to bring a product to market and stuff it through the channel? And yet, they openly admit that the established approaches haven't worked.

At the other end of the food chain there are small start-ups who are trying to establish a market for their 'new, innovative, ground-breaking, paradigm-shifting' product with no marketing resources and with the founders doing the selling. They probably get some early success but more often they falter and never break the $5m revenue barrier.

Most sales and marketing teams do not recognize that there are different buying cultures. They engage every customer against a backdrop of a simple sales process[11]:

- Is there really an opportunity?
- Should we compete?
- Can we win?
- Is this good business?

Every sale is seen as a conquest. There is a winner and a loser. It is a matter of life and death. How many start-ups, after their initial flurry of success, find themselves debating how to grow to the next stage and how many come up with the solution "We will have to hire experienced and expensive salesmen. Who knows any ex-IBMers?"

One Sales Director of a very large software company[12] said to me when he first understood the buying cultures, "I always thought I'd had twenty years of sales experience, I now realize I'd had one experience for twenty years!", i.e. selling to only one buying culture.

[11] Blurred by a healthy dose of testosterone.
[12] Who for obvious reasons preferred to remain anonymous.

FOUR BUYING CULTURES

There are four distinct buying cultures. Each requires a different style of engagement, which are: *Value Offered*, *Value Added*, *Value Created*, and *Value Captured*. We represent them by suits of playing cards.[13]

Fig 1: Your future is in the cards.

First, we need to understand the dynamics of the different buying cultures and agree on some terminology. Imagine that each buying culture is an organization's way of saying to a supplier "This is what I want you to do for me before I actually buy from you."

---

[13] Which seems a better use for cards than losing $1000s in a windowless, soulless casino complex at 3 A.M. in Las Vegas. Yes – I'm not a very good loser.

♥ **Value Captured**: *Why Hearts: Because you're worth it . . . the relationship between supplier and customer is interdependent.*

The Value Captured buying culture occurs when the customer is willing to put themselves in the hands of a supplier in order to generate change or value. An example here would be an organization that is hoping to increase its flexibility and reduce costs through outsourcing. The customer will ultimately share responsibility with the supplier to get the value.

> *Example: Accenture used eBay to sell excess inventory for corporates on a commission-only basis. eBay, the customer, became the supplier as Accenture took all the risks developing the market but reaped the rewards when the 'service' gained momentum.*

♦ **Value Created**: *Why Diamonds: There are diamonds in the rough, but they are difficult for the customer to find.*

The Value Created buying culture occurs when the customer senses there is an opportunity but can't describe it. It takes the supplier to bring it into clear focus and suggest a solution. An example might be an organization that has recognized they need to drive operational effectiveness and improvement, but it takes a supplier to show how they can engage their employees in adopting shared processes, how they will deliver it, and what a solution might look like.

> *Example: Nimbus has been selling its process management software, Control 2007, to manage corporate processes as a valuable asset (as opposed to drawing boxes and lines in Visio). It requires educating customers about its existence and the benefits of the approach and Nimbus Control 2007.*

♠ **Value Added**: *Why Spades: This is about hard work and digging in. Calls multiplied by Demos = Orders! You win 2 out of 5 bids. You negotiate hard and fight for your corner.*

The Value Added buying culture occurs when the customer recognizes that they need to find a solution to a pain or opportunity, and they are looking for options. An example is a customer looking for a CRM system. CRM systems are known to exist and the benefits are understood, but it requires the supplier to explain the value of their product over those of their competitors. The majority of technology is sold in this way. That is why it is usually delegated to the IT department to make the purchase. Alternatively, the business has abdicated responsibility.

Example: SAP competes in the established and understood ERP enterprise software application market. Winning requires better functionality and a lower per seat price in comparison with the other credible competitors.

♣ **Value Offered**: *Why Clubs: You need a club to beat the customer and the competition into submission – it's a commodity/price thing.*

The Value Offered buying culture occurs when the customers know what they want and all that is left to do is decide what color it will be. An example is an organization that is looking to procure a number of laptops as part of an initiative to mobilize the workforce. The customer will conduct his own research and make a decision about which model or version. He will then use the Internet to identify the lowest price or go back to his preferred supplier list. For the supplier it's about establishing a brand and having the lowest friction sales and delivery channel.

Example: Dell laptops are ordered and delivered over the Web and the customer decision is based on Dell's brand, the price, and availability. Dell needs to optimize its supply chain to maintain margins.

HOW DOES ALL THIS RELATE TO GEOFFREY MOORE'S *CHASM?*

There are clear parallels. *Crossing the Chasm* by Geoffrey Moore shows the customer's perspective. Before making any comparisons between sales culture and chasm theory, let's go back to the spot where Geoffrey Moore started, at the theory of Diffusion of Innovation. It's the study of how, why, and at what rate new ideas and technology spread through cultures. This work began in the 1950s at the University of Chicago with funding from television producers who sought a way to measure the effectiveness of broadcast advertising. It soon became apparent that advertised products or services were 'innovations' in the culture. The real pioneer of this thinking was Everett Rogers, who proposed that adopters of any new innovation or idea could be categorized as Innovators (2.5%), Early Adopters (13.5%), Early Majority (34%), Late Majority (34%), and Laggards (16%), based on a bell curve.

Moore argues that there is a chasm between the early adopters of the product (the technology enthusiasts and visionaries) and the early majority (the pragmatists), and these two groups have very different expectations. How does buying culture relate to chasm theory? Fig 2 shows the mapping of buying cultures to chasm theory.

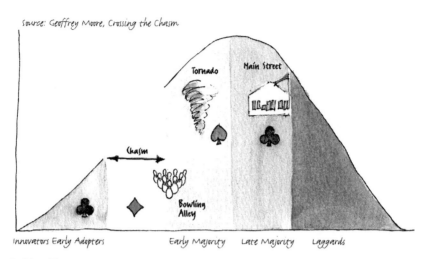

Fig 2: The Chasm

Let's focus on crossing the chasm. That starts with early adopters. The early adopters are people who see breakthrough potential in some technology and want to exploit that potential. Now, some people might believe that the early adopters simply rush straight to purchase. But this is not true. Early adopters follow the same processes of behavior as most other buyers. The big difference is the degree of risk that they are willing to accept as they move through the sales process. Because of this trait they are often quite willing to buy new and unproven technologies as value created buying culture. Quite often it's this initial easy surge of interest from the early adopters which leads a supplier to believe mistakenly that they have a killer product on their hands.

But, early adopters will also buy mature, well-understood products as Value Offered. Selling these products to them using Value Created buying culture simply wastes resources and increases the cost of sale. Crossing the chasm means engaging the early adopters in a Value Created buying culture-driven sale, and then grabbing the attention of the early majority. If the early majority is going to adopt new thinking, they want a 100 percent solution to their business issues. They want a product that works and is supplemented by services and auxiliary products. They want to be able to hire people who've used it. They don't just want a product or point solution. This attitude is typical of the Value Added buying culture. So the product will change buying culture as it crosses the chasm.

Incidentally, Value Captured could be used across any of the buying groups, which is why it's not been shown on the diagram.

WIIFM – SO WHAT EXACTLY DOES ALL THIS MEAN TO ME?

Enough about the customer – what does this mean to you, the supplier? We want to start by looking at the value chain in a very generic fashion. As Fig 3 shows, there are key process silos in the primary value chain and a set of supporting processes.

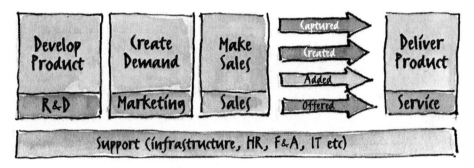

Fig 3: Value Chain & Supporting Processes

The primary value chain starts with product innovation in *Develop Product*, which is where you create, develop, and manufacture your 'products'. It may be a simple piece of hardware or a full service offering. The products are designed, built, polished, and passed over to marketing whose role it is to create messages around the product to *Create Demand* for it. It's the turn of sales to pounce on every opportunity, which they then close and hand over to the delivery teams.[14] In theory, this works very nicely until we factor in the customers' buying cultures, all four of them. We have inserted the four buying cultures between *Make Sales* and *Deliver Product*, because that is where you connect with the customer. Each of the buying cultures is a different route to close business.

What are we saying here? Everything in the business should be focused on the correct route to the customer, based on the way that it wants to buy. But this is not about personal preference, it is driven by the maturity of the product in a given marketplace. For example, a risk-averse customer will not always buy with a Value Captured approach. If the customer needs the benefits of the product described to him by the supplier, the market determines that it will use a Value Added approach.

So, a clear understanding of which buying culture is correct for your product in that particular market and geography is critical. Choose the wrong route and your killer product will stall before it starts and the entire value chain will be wrong. R&D will not be responsive to changes and updates. Marketing will spend a great deal of money projecting the wrong messages. Sales commission plans will not encourage the right behavior. Sales people will be incentivized to take the wrong route.[15]

At this point you might be tempted to think "Well, the answer is easy. This is just about understanding the quirky behavior of the customers and getting our sales guys to match their behaviors." But this is not simply a sales issue, it is an issue that the whole organization needs to address. It is about the creation and alignment of the operational culture of your company.

---

[14] Pausing only to collect the commission and bask in the glory of another sale won.
[15] When sales guys are branded 'short term-focused' it means that they have a Value Added/Offered sales commission structure which forces that behavior.

Alignment of the supplier's operational culture and the customer's buying culture is the fundamental key to the success of a product.

Alignment of the supplier's operational culture and the customer's buying culture addresses such issues as:

- The product – is it innovative or me-too?
- The target market – is it sensitive or commoditized?
- The sales force – product or concept?
- Sales commission and company incentives – what is the product margin or likelihood of company success?
- The partner ecosystem – will it generate demand or deliver solutions?
- The competition – is it complacent or aggressive?
- Brand equity – is it positive or irrelevant?

What we do see from this perspective is that the customers' buying cultures need to be taken into consideration within all elements of the value chain when creating, designing, and building that killer product. It affects the cultural feel of the company. It touches every area of the business.

So, to understand how to develop the correct operational culture, we need to look into how an organization buys in a lot more detail. What is the process that it goes through? How are decisions made? And how does this decision-making process fit with the buying cultures?

HOW DO PEOPLE BUY?

Strictly speaking, the title of this section should be 'How organizations buy' as this is really a book about business-to-business sales. However, since it is individuals within those organizations who buy from other individuals, we would be naïve to consider corporate culture without looking at it through the eyes of the different personalities of the buyers. For example, a company full of infectious, over-optimistic entrepreneurial types will purchase differently from those in a risk-averse government department.

That said, there is a pathway or process that all organizations follow to reach purchasing decisions. This process does not vary across industries or even regions of the world, because it is inextricably linked to instinctive human behavior. It is just the speed that organizations or individuals travel through the process that differs. The process is called IMPACT.

The IMPACT process may be followed in a formal way or it may be tacit and informal. It may involve large numbers of people, both inside and outside the organization, or it may be driven by one individual. It is guaranteed that any idea which leads to a purchase in an organization, be it corporately or personally driven, has followed this process.

The six key phases of the process are easy to remember as they have an enormous IMPACT on your company's performance:

Identify – Mentor – Position – Assessment – Case – Transaction

Every purchase goes through all six phases, with or without the supplier's assistance. What differs between the four different buying cultures is the point at which the supplier is given permission to engage with the customer. The reason that most salesmen don't recognize this process is because the customer goes through the process on their own, and only invites the supplier in for the last one or two steps. But more of this later. First, let's understand the IMPACT process.

Phase 1: Identify

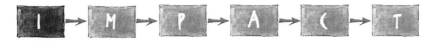

The identification of ideas for changing or improving a business that are good enough to warrant investigation.

This is the ideas phase. This may be the executive team going on an off-site with strategic consultants to plan its future. The executive team will be looking for ways to grow revenues, create competitive advantage, increase shareholder value, contain or reduce costs. That is, it is 'blue sky' thinking to discover breakout ideas, rather than looking for solutions. Alternatively, it could be looking out into the future to see how technology will help the company become more competitive or impact its markets.

Phase 2: Mentor

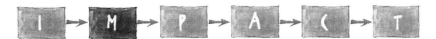

Enrolling a mentor (evangelist) to the idea to validate it.

The executive team will take the breakthrough ideas or big bets and give them to someone in senior management to act as a mentor for the ideas. These ideas are not for public consumption, and the mentor should only work with his close team and trusted advisors to ratify the thinking. The mentor will be scoping and testing the ideas for feasibility, credibility, and political acceptability as much as he can without drawing undue attention. Mentors may send out a Request for Information (RFI) to test the market at this point. The mentor will produce a report which will be presented back to the executive team. If accepted, the mentor will start to plan how the breakthrough idea can be delivered as an initiative, how it will be announced, what will be presented and to whom, and a route through the expected political maze. A sponsor may have aligned himself with the initiative – either formally or informally.

If the report is not accepted then the ideas get buried – forever.

Phase 3: Position

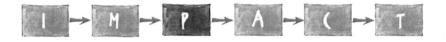

The public decision to make resources and budget available to invest further in the idea.

Buy-in is the big challenge because it involves managing politics. But why do politics play such a major part in this phase? The answer is simple. The announcement of a new initiative is an announcement of impending change. And change will always produce an upsurge of emotions, both positive and negative. Executives know that the moment they announce a new initiative they will see their teams form into camps – those who are for it, those who are against it, and those who are trying to take credit for it. So, what happens in this phase? Once the initiative is announced the mentor will be responsible for all the communications from this point. But the mentor will need to find a sponsor, because to move forward into the next phase will require resources (money, people, time) to assess the value of the initiative. The sponsor will be the person or body of people with enough political muscle to get the resources. Remember when Carly Fiorina announced to the Packard family shareholders that she intended to acquire Compaq? They rejected her idea out of hand and at that point her idea was dead, unless she could find herself a sponsor with more power than the Packard family. She found this in the form of the institutional investors on Wall Street. The mentor will know that the initiative is moving out of the Position phase when an assessment team is assigned.

Phase 4: Assessment

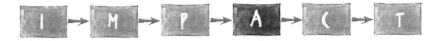

The assessment of the good and the bad in the idea.

The Assessment phase plays a very important part in the post-Enron corporate world. In the 1990s, corporate accountability and due diligence were seen as overhead or optional. Enron, Tyco International, Adelphia, WorldCom, and others changed that. These scandals, which cost investors billions of dollars and shook public confidence, generated legislation that ensures company officers are held accountable for their decisions. Particularly ones involving investment and strategic direction, which has made the Assessment phase a big hurdle.[16] But the Assessment phase is not about cost justification, it is an evaluation of everything, both quantitative and qualitative. This typically involves an assessment team or project team conducting a proof of concept or pilot project to generate the evidence and data. Hence, the need for a sponsor capable of funding the team.

Phase 5: Case

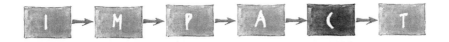

The creation of a quantified business case and assignment of resources/ budget to it.

---

[16] And some executives would see this as personal insurance, keeping them out of prison.

The mentor will use the output from the Assessment phase to build a business and investment Case, possibly including solutions. It's likely that this Case will then be pushed back and forth between the mentor and the sponsor until the sponsor is happy that the Case appears to support all relevant business and political goals. Then, the Case can have a budget actually assigned to it and will be made public. If the organization requires that all external purchases are done via competitive tender, then this is when those tender documents are created and distributed.

Phase 6: Transaction

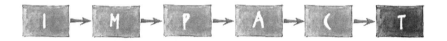

The confirmation of the project to all internal and external stakeholders and to the suppliers.

Procurement will raise a purchase order and negotiate contracts for the solution put forward in the Case. Depending on the solution, market and company approach procurement may need to drive a formal procurement with competitive tendering, beauty parades, and all the fun and games that this entails.

MOMENTUM = GETTING THE RIGHT PEOPLE ON BOARD

The fuel which keeps the IMPACT process moving is the sense of importance of the original idea, at both a corporate and personal level. Corporate politics will also play a role. The importance of personal and political goals must never be under-rated, because they are often backed by 'alpha'-type personalities. These are people who have gained the loyalty and attention of others throughout the company. It may be because they are respected, feared, successful, manipulative, and control access to some critical business process – or all of the above. The sense of importance that these alphas will be able to attach to the idea will be significant. These people have significant power because they are good at spotting and supporting good ideas.[17]

MANAGING RISK

The idea remains at risk at every phase in the process. Most of the risk lies in the initiative or product being rationalized as not valid for the company at that time (i.e., it's a bad idea). Hence, it will be ditched at one phase or another. But the idea is at risk between each phase for a variety of other reasons:

- Political – the internal politics of the customer.
- Product – whether the product being considered is 'proven'.
- Value – what is the pure business value of the idea?
- Financial – whether the idea creates unacceptable liabilities or costs too much.
- Brand – is the idea and any product in keeping with the image of the customer, is it 'on brand'?

All of this means that any idea can be dropped at any phase of the IMPACT process, but the phase which presents the greatest risk to the supplier is Position, which is the graveyard of many ideas and poorly aligned suppliers. This is because it is during this phase that you, as a supplier, are most at risk of having your value stolen. Think about it, if you engage at the Mentor phase with an opinion about the customer's idea, at that point it is just you and one or two others having a 'conversation of possibilities'. The idea (which is now linked with your product) is accepted and goes public. You are then in a world of swirling emotions where the company politicians, empire builders, and plagiarists[18] live.

---

[17] What is power without control? [Pirelli tyre advert]
[18] Plagiarism is where you steal an idea. If you steal multiple ideas you can call it 'research'.

Any, or all, of them may think about making a name for themselves by stealing the idea, but they will need to align with another supplier. Your role as the supplier during the Position phase is to identify all risks and the people attached to them, mitigate the risks, and then move the idea and the mentor into the relatively safe waters of the Assessment phase as quickly as possible.

CHAPTER 3

If they are buying – are you selling?

CHOOSING THE CORRECT BUYING CULTURE

A question we get asked a lot is, "Which buying culture should I choose, and which is the best?" Firstly, you don't choose how you want to sell. The customer, or rather the maturity of the product in a marketplace, determines the buying culture at a point in time. All you get to choose is how you react and organize yourselves – what we will call your *operational culture*. The smart money is in being able to determine which buying cultures you need to support or align to. Note, we said buying cultures – plural. If you have a range of products then it's highly likely that you will be supporting multiple operational cultures.[19]

A clear understanding of the buying culture of a customer leads to a clear realization that the entire organization needs to be aligned to mirror that buying culture. But what is the benefit of driving an aligned operational culture? The answer is that if you can align the core processes of both the primary and secondary value chains to the correct operational culture, you will be able to optimize sales. As a result, your killer product will become just that – a killer product.

---

[19] And even before you know what an operational culture is, having more than one sounds like bad news.

Operational culture affects far more than just the sales team.

As you will see in the examples, we are talking about the entire organization's orientation to an operational culture to mirror the customer's buying culture. R&D, Marketing, Sales, Sales Operations, Professional Services, Support & Help Desk, Legal, and Alliances are all affected. The only functions that are innocent bystanders are HR, IT, and Finance.

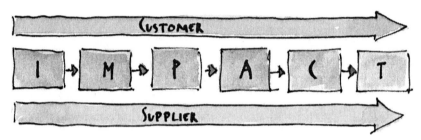

Fig 4: Customer and Supplier IMPACT Cycle.

Earlier we said that each of the buying cultures has a different entry point for the supplier as the customer navigates through the IMPACT process. Below are the different buying cultures overlaid on the IMPACT process. We can now start to explore what it will feel like for the supplier when engaging with each of the buying cultures.

All sales engagements are founded on 'delivering value'. Value may be increasing future revenues, maintaining current revenues, or reducing or avoiding costs for the customer. If the customer is in the public sector then it could be increasing services and service levels, or reducing or avoiding costs.

Two questions for any engagement are:

- Who has responsibility for **recognizing** where the potential value is in the supplier's product?

- Who has responsibility for actually **delivering** the value of the supplier's product for the customer?

It may be that the customer is responsible for recognizing that there is value in a product and is responsible for the successful implementation of the product. Or it may be that the supplier identifies the value for the customer, but it's still then the customer that is on the hook to deliver. Finally, there is the situation where the supplier sees the value and is responsible for delivering the value. The approach to be taken will be decided by the buying culture and will be evident in the contract between the customer and the supplier.

EXPLORING THE BUYING CULTURES

Let's explore how each of the buying cultures feels from a supplier's sales engagement perspective, starting with Value Captured.

Value Captured

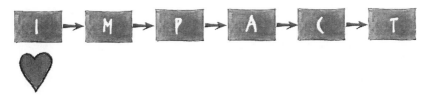

If the customer is at the Identify stage it is likely that they are making themselves aware of the major change issues in their world. But the supplier will probably know more about the issues for the customer than they do. This is partly because the Value Captured supplier's product will have the capability of driving change if not actually *being* the change itself. If the supplier is branded as a change agent, it's likely that they will be invited in by the customer to help study their options. Marketing will focus on insight through white papers, conferences, and maintaining high visibility with business and organizational leaders. So, the supplier is responsible for recognizing the value of their product for the customer. The supplier is likely to be responsible for the delivery of that value within the sales engagement – i.e., the supplier is paid based on the success of the customer. Quite often, the contracting approach is Joint Venture or the UK's Private Finance Initiative.[20]

A good example of this is Accenture. Back in 2002 they spotted the opportunity to use eBay to sell excess inventory for corporates, giving them 20 percent higher prices than dumping them through their normal channels. Up to this point eBay was an 'electronic car boot sale' for individuals. Accenture took responsibility for developing the market, recruiting corporate sellers, and were paid a commission on all sales. eBay assumed no risk, but received a proportionally smaller revenue share. It rapidly turned into a multimillion pound revenue stream for both eBay and Accenture.

CUSTOMER ATTRIBUTES	SUPPLIER ATTRIBUTES
• Not risk-averse, but not necessarily entrepreneurial	• Entrepreneurial
• Able to run risk–reward or JV projects	• Able to run risk–reward or JV projects
• Able to license IP to third parties	• Well funded
	• High integrity

[20] This is the UK Government getting industry to develop a product or solution and lease it back to the Government – such as a bridge, a school, hospital, or computer system.

Value Created

The customer is studying its strategic options. The starting point for sales here is the perspective that the supplier has of the customer's market, organization, culture, operations, and strategy. The supplier will be able to see things that the customer cannot possibly see itself, so the sales engagement is more likely to be initiated by the supplier and supported by thought-leadership marketing and industry insights. The customer will not be out looking for a supplier because it probably doesn't realize that a product exists to satisfy a requirement that it is only just realizing it has.

The supplier needs to find a mentor for its product. The supplier will need to grab the attention of the mentor with an opinion about the customer's organization, and issues in the customer's market. Early meetings will be a 'conversation of possibilities' and not a discussion of products or solutions. As the engagement progresses, the supplier will help the customer understand how to exploit its products. But the product's existence is not well understood by all customers, which causes an unhealthy tension between the business and IT in technology sales. The business side of the customer sees something that it wants to buy, with or without their IT department's blessing. There are few, if any, other directly competing products and no third-party assessment. The market isn't sufficiently developed for the analysts to create a comparison matrix. Therefore, IT will be uncomfortable with purchasing it. And they may even block it.

An example of a product in this area is Nimbus Control 2007, which is an application for capturing end-to-end processes and publishing them as an organization's Operations Manual. This is delivered through their intranet, dynamically, with links to metrics, documents, and applications. Quite often an alternative product is used to satisfy the business need. But as it has not been designed to meet the real need, it is not a complete solution. As a known alternative to Nimbus Control 2007, in 90 percent of cases Microsoft Visio is used for mapping processes. Despite Visio's limitations around publishing and version control, the customer soldiers on because it doesn't realize there is a better-suited product in the market. Therefore, Nimbus needs to educate the market before it can sell to it, and it also needs to establish itself as a thought-leader, requiring it to develop a strong professional services practice to support its product.

CUSTOMER ATTRIBUTES	SUPPLIER ATTRIBUTES
• Picks winners	• Business-focused
• Methodical	• Good partner ecosystem
• Intuitive	• Consultative, visionary, thought leader
• Contrarian and risk-taker	• Not driven by short-term commission

Value Added

Products are well known and there is a broad understanding of their capabilities. Therefore customers, once they have established their needs, are able to source possible solutions. The really important thing about a Value Added customer is that they have a recognized and quantified need or pain or opportunity. The supplier needs to ensure that its profile, driven by traditional advertising and marketing, is high enough so that it is contacted by customers. The supplier will engage the customer at the

Case phase. The sales people will be trained in interpersonal sales skills, so that they can quickly establish the pain points and handle objections. The role of sales is to qualify the customers and add value by using knowledge of the products to build a solution which will meet the customers' needs and be differentiated from their competitors. Whilst the customer is still at the Case stage, the sales people will have a bit of flexibility to gather more information and demonstrate their solution. Once the customer moves to the Transaction stage, they will be locked into a 'best and finals' process with little or no flexibility.

Once the solution has been specified, designed, and priced, the sales person does not want to accept any responsibility for the realization of value from the solution – his job is done once the deal is closed.

The majority of business software such as CRM, ERP, or Accounting is bought in this way. This is where IT has been delegated to make the purchase, or the business has abdicated responsibility. A classic example of this is Oracle or SAP. The customer will have identified the business need and compiled a list of requirements. They then use third-party advice, such as from an analyst, research, or a consulting firm, to draw up a short-list of suppliers. Normally, the market leader and three to four others will appear on the short-list. Then, there is a formal proposal/bidding process to select the winner, which is decided on the balance of functionality vs. price.

CUSTOMER ATTRIBUTES	SUPPLIER ATTRIBUTES
• Pragmatic and picks market leaders	• Quarterly- or monthly-focused
• Organized and disciplined	• Good customer qualification process
• Decisive	• Focused technical support
• Good project management	• Competitively savvy

Value Offered

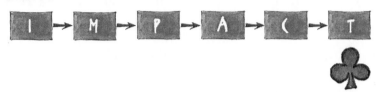

What is the customer doing? It knows what it wants and is looking at the choices. This engagement is very much as it sounds – where the role of sales is to get the product out there, and cover as much ground as possible with short, sharp engagements. The product needs to be of a nature such that the customer can easily understand where the value is for them, because there is not the margin for a field salesman to have to explain anything beyond features. All the responsibility for recognizing where the value is in the product lies with the customer. In Value Offered we will only want to engage with the customer when it's quite clear what is wanted, solutions are already defined, and budgets and time frames are quite clear. The leads will come from marketing and direct sales activity, which will probably be some kind of inside sales organization. The marketing angle will typically be the price-to-feature leverage. The engagement takes place when the customer is in the Transactions phase. Customers only want to deal with the market leaders, provided they are cost-competitive, so brand value and recognition is everything.

Dell is the perfect example on PCs and laptops. It established a superior product build and delivery model and was able to drive down prices to enable it to gain market share. Interestingly, when Dell tried to apply this to the server market, which is still a Value Added market, the Value Offered model didn't work – which is why you see Dell changing its operating model for server sales.

CUSTOMER ATTRIBUTES	SUPPLIER ATTRIBUTES
• Resolute	• Strong, recognized brand
• Good governance	• Gorilla
• Strong negotiator	• Energetic and aggressive
• Cost-conscious/cheapskates	• Aware of margin

DIFFERENT BUYING CULTURES, DIFFERENT OPERATIONAL CULTURES

An easy way to highlight the differences between the different buying cultures is to look at various attributes of the company. Look at how they develop new business, the company culture, and how they partner. The following table highlights the differences, but the table is not a definitive answer. It should give you clues about where you should be positioning your products.

You should be able to position each of your products against a buying culture based on the attributes in the table above. You will also be able to determine your company's dominant selling approach.

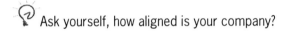 Ask yourself, how aligned is your company?

ATTRIBUTE	VALUE CAPTURED	VALUE CREATED	VALUE ADDED	VALUE OFFERED
Brand (How well established/known is the brand?)	Established in sector/industry	Quirky, alternative, and highly memorable	500lb gorilla in the market	Household name. Top of the search engines
Sales creativity (How innovative are the sales team?)	Entrepreneurial	Proactive	Reactive	Demand-driven
R&D (Product design and manufacture)	Reuse/reapply existing product analytics	These are solutions Jim, but not as we know them	Driving the next wave	Driving margin improvement and stability
Market (What state is the market in?)	Change-driven	Sensitive (for whatever reason)	Demand-led	Commoditized
Product offering (What are you offering the customer?)	Risk-free	Business solution	Technical solutions	One-dimensional
Value proposition (What is the value to the customer?)	Holistic	Issue-focused	Feature-focused	Price-focused
Business development (How do we generate qualified leads?)	Personal networks	Thought-leadership	Marketing machine	Search engine optimized

	Part of the joint team	Long-term revenue stream	Respond to RFPs	Preferred supplier
Sales motivation (What drives our salesmen?)	Part of the joint team	Long-term revenue stream	Respond to RFPs	Preferred supplier
Customer (What is our relationship?)	Interdependent	Empathetic	Transactional	Superficial
Sales contacts (At what level!?)	Board	Executive	Users	Technical
Sales planning (How do we engage?)	A mutual plan based on the markets	An account plan focused on the customer's current risk model	An aggregated call plan reacting to the customer's needs	A contact plan covering schedules, renewals, and product push
Sales relationship (What attitude do they bring to work?)	Counselor	Consultant	Work rate and tenacity	Thick skin
Key channels (What is route to market?)	Strategy consultants	Systems integrators	Value added resellers	Fulfillment and distribution
Business risks (What are the risks to the supplier?)	Cash flow	Long-term revenue stream	Cost of sale	Margin
Competition (Who is eating my lunch?)	No-one, but fear and apathy in the customer	Alternative approaches	500lb gorillas and random monkeys	Anyone with the same product
Teaming (How to establish teams within supplier?)	Dynamic	Virtual	Individual	Internally competitive
Network (What is supplier–salesmen network?)	Holistic	External	Internal	Restricted

WHAT DOES A VALUE CAPTURED COMPANY FEEL LIKE?

♥ **Value Captured**: The supplier shares full risk and reward by capturing the value jointly with the customer.

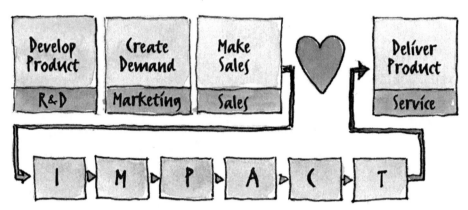

Fig 5: Value Captured value chain

Culture

Massively entrepreneurial. Enough to give any corporate CFO a sleepless night, unless the company is extremely well funded or is a subsidiary of a very understanding or entrepreneurial group company.

Business model

Every business model is different. It is based on the deal struck between the customer and the supplier. Although at times it could seem that the relationship between the customer and the supplier has been reversed. It could be a Joint Venture (JV), a commission paid to the customer for the use of the product or service, equity ownership and earn out, or purchase lease back. You name it. Anything goes. This is the area of financial innovation.

Metrics

Overall value increases – whatever that means in the context of the business model and deal. It could be profit, brand, revenue, or CEO's ego.[21] The classic metrics for a Value Captured company are the operational Service Level Agreements (SLAs) that they agree with their customer and on which they will make their money.

R&D

These development guys don't tend to be the technologists. They are more likely to be market analysts, financial analysts, and futurologists. They will be looking to predict or create the next wave of business behavior and capitalize on it – early.

Marketing

Value Captured marketing will most likely be carried out behind the closed doors of an invitation-only seminar or a private club. Traditional marketing is not what is needed to develop the relationship between customer and supplier. In fact, the ability to drive the maximum return out of the relationship requires that no-one else spots the market opportunity.[22]

Sales

Who makes the initial engagement? It is normally the supplier, seeing an under-exploited opportunity for a customer. But the sales team is really a deal team made up of sales, commercial, and legal people. Very often the toughest sale is back inside the supplier company, to get the idea accepted internally and funded.

---

[21] JVs are just like M&A – deal-making – and CEOs love doing deals. However, JVs are potentially safer as they can be ring-fenced.
[22] A Non Disclosure Agreement (NDA) is the only piece of marketing collateral.

Delivery

Delivery is completely dependent on the nature of the deal.

Best for

A change-driven marketplace subjected to disruptive markets. The business model pushes radically new approaches to business and organizational management, but is not necessarily the world of bleeding-edge technology.

WHAT DOES A VALUE CREATED COMPANY FEEL LIKE?

◆ **Value Created:** The supplier reveals unforeseen risk or opportunity for the customer (thus creating new value for them) and will assume some kind of responsibility to realize the return.

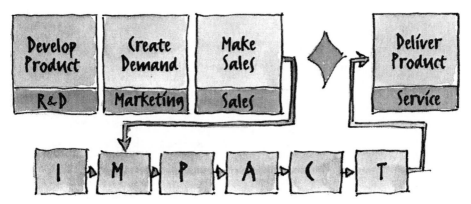

Fig 6: Value Created value chain

Culture

The whole company is genuinely customer-focused. Not in the false sense of *"our customer is our No. 1 focus – Your call is really important to us, please hold for 10 minutes . . ."* I'm talking about a really deep interest in the customer and their world. Your professional services and sales team are expected to live in the customer world to the extent that they understand the emotional highs and lows of the customer. They are part of the furniture at the customer. They count the customers as friends. This is the world where the account manager takes customers out to lunch whether there is business on the table or not.

Business model

The big thing here is to grab the customer's attention and then, once it's grabbed, hold onto it forever. Then somehow get a project started with

43

your innovative, disruptive technology, solution or approach. Once established in the customer, the target is to expand virally until you have sufficient momentum to wrap them up completely and then feast on the resulting revenue stream.

There will be a high level of professional services in the early days to help the customer be successful. So much so that you will constantly be asked "Are we a consulting firm or a product company?"[23] We remember endless debates at SAS Institute and Nimbus about whether they were software companies with a professional services team or consulting firms with very clever tools.

Relationships with customers will be deep and long-term. That means they may take 12–18 months before the initial sales activity 'breaks even' in terms of product sales. So, the revenue stream is a combination of product and professional services. The focus is on revenue growth, where each new customer takes some time before the long sales cycle shows a return. Because of the longer sales cycle you must be very aware of resource usage through the cycle, so the partner ecosystem assumes new importance here.

Metrics

The metrics for Value Created focus as much on progression as on results. This means a well-balanced mix of leading and lagging indicators. Some of the metrics may include:

- Revenue growth by customer vs. cost of sales.
- Number of sector marketing initiatives which make it to Assessment phase per customer.
- Number of supplier sales and professional services staff have a security pass for their customer, so they can roam freely.

[23] With the natural concerns about valuation of the company from the investors.

Traditional CRM systems have difficulty handling this kind of measurement.[24]

R&D

The R&D teams are innovative with short release cycles to be able to respond to customer demands. The solution does not need to be 100 percent completed. 70 percent will do, with a commitment to work with the customer to discover what the other 30 percent should be.

Marketing

These guys will be seen as strategic thought-leadership. Their primary task is to create sector-based initiatives driving interest around just-current or future issues in any given sector. They will educate the market with books, articles, and seminars rather than advertising, PR, and direct mail. In some companies they may be tasked with making the primary engagement with the customer on a Value Created issue.

Sales

The entire organization – or at least the group supporting the Value Created sale – is entirely customer-focused. It's difficult to tell the difference between the sales guys and the consultants – in fact, they can operate interchangeably. The only difference is that the sales guys are commissioned. Paradoxically, the consultants are better salesmen than consultants, as they are trusted by the customers. Nurturing the customer and demanding their attention is their first task. This is done by initially finding the mentor and then supporting him internally, normally on a day-rate. If your mentor has zero budget, or does not have access to budget at a later date, then he doesn't count as a true mentor. Early work could be running internal seminars and constantly being available to do demos without any expectation of an immediate sale. The aim is to generate an internal viral campaign,

---

[24] As do old-school, meat-eating Value Added Sales Directors.

orchestrated and resourced under the radar by your mentor. The more senior the mentor is, the higher the 'under-the-radar' budget will be.

The help desk staff have a part to play as they know the customers well and can operate as junior consultants. In fact, this is a career progression; from help desk to consultant, on to pre-sales and then sales.

Delivery

Early-stage projects probably look more like consulting engagements with some limited product sales. But as the customer matures they will rely on the consultants less and less.

Best for

The table at the beginning of this section says this is the world of the sensitive market, but you are probably still wondering what is meant by that. *Sensitive* might apply to emerging technologies or markets that are going through a time of flux themselves. Value Created is for customers that need their investments to be de-risked.

WHAT DOES A VALUE ADDED COMPANY LOOK LIKE?

♠ **Value Added**: *The supplier responds to the customer's needs or pain and uses its knowledge (adds value) of its products and services to build a solution.*

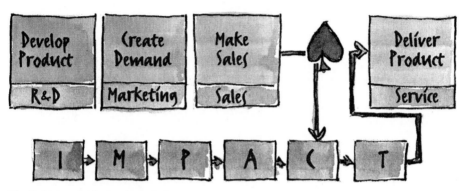

Fig 7: Value Added value chain

Culture

The executive team of a Value Added company would like to think that they were Value Created – thought-leaders with the customers hanging upon their every word, but without all the hard work and complication involved. A long-term relationship without the courting. The reality is very different. Value Added companies are in a fiercely competitive marketplace trying to differentiate themselves from other, similar-looking products. The management style in the Value Added world will tend to be command and control. A blend of macho sales and heroics in delivery.

Business model

Field-based product sales. Winning proposals against the 'usual suspects' competition. Trying to outsmart the competition on features and functions.

47

Trying to get closer to the customer without burning too much free pre-sales consulting. Maximizing margin on every deal. Consulting is a necessary evil, and a profit center. The support desk and training are also profit centers, and may have their own sales teams and targets. Sales guys live or die by their numbers. Discounting at the end of each quarter is rife to close a deal. Therefore, most deals are done in the last five days of a quarter.[25]

Metrics

The metrics are profit, revenue, margin per salesman, and proposal win rate. Traditional sales forecasting works.

R&D

Product development is all about maximizing margin. Product features are targeted at a release to ensure that the product is stable, will scale, and returns are minimized. The product is 'complete' or it would be impossible to compete and win.

Marketing

Marketing is all about brand awareness in front of the target customers. That means advertising, junk email, web ads, webinars, seminars, and PR. In the Value Added world, taking the customer out to lunch is seen as an aspect of marketing and so will only be done when there is a deal on the table, and the tables can be turned on the competition.

Sales

The key intention and mindset of the Value Added sales person is to do deals, make sales, and hit the numbers. Their environment will be heavily

[25] Or in the last 10 days of the financial year.

geared towards doing this. Compensation will be deal- and revenue-linked. Recognition will be for those who hit their numbers. Heroes or zeros.

Once they have used their knowledge to develop a solution from their own products, structured a deal, and signed a contract, the Value Added salesmen will disengage. Delivery is someone else's problem. They've collected their commission. Next.

The core skills will be traditional sales skills: questioning, objection handling, tool-based negotiation, and proposal presentation. The IQ for Value Added sales people is that they can build pipeline and drive their way through it. The EQ for Value Added sales people is that they must have a strong work rate and a thick skin. They will engage with the necessary management who can explain the customer's pain or need. Value Added people may meet with more senior people, but since they will have no relevance to them there will be no relationship.

Delivery

Delivery is a cost center. It may be subcontracted or sold and delivered by third parties. It will be repeatable, risk-free, and profitable.

Best for

Demand-led markets where there is an established, known need.

WHAT DOES A VALUE OFFERED COMPANY LOOK LIKE?

♣ **Value offered**: *The supplier makes the products available (thus offering the value). The customer or partner applies their own knowledge to exploit them.*

Fig 8: Value Offered value chain

Doesn't this picture look tempting with such a short sales cycle!

Culture

One cannot say that all Value Offered companies have the same culture, but they do follow a trend of being very numbers-driven, gung-ho, focused on the individual, praising the hero of sales. Not necessarily 'Pile it high and sell it cheap', but focused on volume as margins will be razor thin.[26] Management style will most likely be supervisory. Staff satisfaction is low and therefore staff turnover is high.

Business model

Clean and simple is the answer. Streamlined.[27] If we look at the value chain for a Value Offered company we will see that everything from

---

[26] Unless it's consulting – yes, consulting is often sold using a Value Offered model. The consulting days are a commodity. An expensive one.

[27] Like a shark rather than a dolphin. Predatory rather than intellectual.

product innovation right through to service delivery is clean and simple, and designed to extract as much money as possible from every transaction. We don't want the customer's buying process to get in our way or complicate things at all. The product will in no way involve leading-edge technology; everything about it is known, tried, and tested.

Metrics

Clean and simple again. Number of units shipped, product revenues, field sales calls per week, demos per month, number of tender documents submitted, and finally success rate. Inside sales performance measures would be similar: calls per day, average duration of calls, and average revenue per call.

R&D

R&D is optimized for high-volume, low-margin, zero returns. Any color as long as it's black. Customization or options are products, purchased separately and fitted during delivery.

Marketing

Marketing will drive the name and the brand. All messages will be features-focused, building up the value of the product, playing on the brand, and emphasizing the ease with which the product can be acquired and deployed.

Sales

Sales will be very light-touch, possibly using only the Internet or inside sales teams. Field sales people are hired not for their ability to create relationships, but to cover ground. They will be managing a large territory of customers, either geographically or within an industry. Very often a sales engagement will be started by the issuing of a tender document by the customer. However the sales cycle starts, it needs to be kept short because margin will always be at risk in the Value Offered model.

The sales person has only one intention, which is to get you to order his product or service. Typically, their core skills will be telephone-handling, scripting, basic presentation and demonstration.

Delivery

Delivery may be through a third-party network or the customer themselves. To be honest, the supplier isn't really worried. There are plenty more customers where you came from.

Best for

Commoditized markets.

CHAPTER 4

The best kept secret – Value Created sales

WHY VALUE CREATED

In this chapter we are going to address in some depth the challenge of creating and maintaining a Value Created operational culture. From what you've read so far you will realize it isn't that easy. But you may be asking, why focus on Value Created as opposed to any of the other three? The answer is that from years of consulting we've learned that Value Offered, Value Added, and Value Captured are all obvious sales entry points for suppliers. However, Value Created is very rarely used because it is not understood. It is almost always mistaken for 'Value Added, but where the salesmen are a bit more consultative'. Yet, Value Created is the only effective way of selling innovative or disruptive products, and is very different from Value Added. It has a different process, runs at a different rhythm, and requires a different set of personalities. The transition to Value Created is the most needed and most difficult.

Often the differences between Value Created and Value Added are subtle.

A salesman could be lucky and find that perfect customer, so his Value Added approach worked when really a Value Created one should have been used. With long sales cycles the results are not seen for some time, but it's unlikely that even the best sales person can be successful long term if they are selling against the wrong buying culture. However, based on the competitiveness and testosterone surrounding sales, I've never seen a salesman admit he has a poor sales approach.[28]

For most products in a maturing marketplace, or a demand-led market, the buying culture is Value Added. Think enterprise software such as ERP and CRM, or in the hardware space with servers and routers. So when a product hits the mainstream, it's Value Added. This is where there are large companies with huge sales teams. We remember in the heyday of the 1990s one Sales Director at Sun Microsystems describing selling as easy, like "standing next to a fire hydrant with a bucket!" Therefore, the vast bulk of the pool of salesmen is going to be steeped in the Value Added sales approach. Good at presenting, qualification, questioning, and proposal-writing. So if a new innovative product is launched it is likely that the 'proven' sales people who are hired will approach the problem of selling it from a Value Added perspective. And they will fail – eventually. But because they were hired for their track record, they are unlikely to question themselves.

So, the fundamental issue we see in company after company is that Value Added is the default operational culture when it really should be Value Created.

---

[28] This is rather like admitting that he's a bad driver, or a lousy lover.

WHY DO SO MANY COMPANIES GET IT WRONG?

So if this is so obvious, why do so many companies get it wrong? Simple. When the new start-up or division is put together, or a new company and its products are acquired, the difference between Value Created and Value Added is never known.[29] So the entire business model is geared around Value Added selling, based on:

- Salesmen aim for big software sales from the get-go. Just like the other products in maturing markets.
- Big sales guys with strong track records are hired, and their incentives reinforce the wrong behaviors.
- The sales support infrastructure – help desk, pre-sales, and professional services – are not in place.
- The metrics inside the company and from the shareholders are driving the wrong operational culture.

But the biggest reason for failure is that: 'Value Created is a myth'.

The perspective of a salesman is "I have built a 20-year career in successful technology sales (i.e., Value Added). I have been recruited into a new division with an innovative product or lured into a start-up as the 'sales god'." They are not going to question themselves, their proven track record, or their approach. "Sack me or back me" is their taunt, or threat, to the executive team. High testosterone Value Added sales guys see Value Created as simply a sales technique they should apply. They think that they should be more consultative in their approach. They don't or can't see that there is a very different underlying process they need to apply. Often the only change management technique that will work with these people is humor.[30] Later on we will look at the different attributes of great Value Created salesmen vs. great Value Added salesmen.

---

[29] If it were, there wouldn't be a need for this book or all our training and consulting.
[30] Knock, knock. Who's there? Not you any more . . . (i.e., you fire them).

So, does that mean you are getting it wrong? We need to clarify what we mean by "getting it wrong". Wrong means wrong for the customer. So wrong can apply to many things: wrong product placement, wrong marketing message, wrong sales incentives, wrong sales people, wrong brand equity, wrong measurements, wrong culture, wrong partners, or just simply the whole lot wrong.

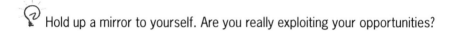

Hold up a mirror to yourself. Are you really exploiting your opportunities?

But what we see is salesmen underperforming due to a misalignment between the sales engagement and the buying culture. So let's look at the potential misalignment, which occurs between adjacent buying cultures. Rather like the distinct buyers not being clearly understood until Geoffrey Moore called them out, the difference between the different buying cultures are not apparent until they are clearly articulated. Then the light bulb goes on.

VITAL SIGNS

Remember, it is the product that determines which buying culture, and hence which operational culture, is required. More precisely, it is the product in a specific market which determines the buying culture. So how can you decide if your product requires a Value Created buying culture or not?

First, take a look at the table in Chapter 3 and see if you can identify where you are. If that on its own doesn't work, then what are the vital signs that you should be looking for? Remember that when a market matures the buying culture flips from Value Created to Value Added. Then the whole operation needs to be reoriented or it will become very unprofitable. First, let's look for the vital signs that suggest you should be selling as Value Created, in the table and then explore them in more detail.

VITAL SIGNS	THE COVER UP: THE SALESMAN'S SELF-DECEPTION
Market maturity	It's great. We've got no competition. We should clean up.
Multiple buyers	It's not a problem. Everyone across the business, in every division, is interested.
Sales stalled	We're really close now. We've got so many companies about to sign.
Pilots, no pull-through	The last pilot was a huge success. So much so that they want to pilot in another area.
Small incremental sales	Most customers are not committing to large orders, for anything.
Multiple products mask and confuse sales effort	The sales team's not a problem. Some of the products are going gangbusters.
Multiple products but only one sales team	No-one is going to be selling to my customer. I own the account.
Brand recognition (or aspirations) not aligned with product mix	We operate at Board level. What more do you want?
Run out of mates and early adopters to sell to	We've proven we can do this. Look at the sales history. Marketing needs to pull its finger out and get us better leads.
How interesting is your product?	We've got a winner. Everyone we talk to is really, really interested.

Market maturity

How mature is the product in a specific marketplace? One sign is that there is relatively little (if any) competition. You can always construct a scenario for any product where there is no competition, i.e. "We sell a kennel designed for dogs that are less than four feet long and 18 inches high and prefer to sleep on a feather down rug." What we mean is that in the eyes of the buyer there is not a natural alternative that you are compared against.

This means that you are rarely bidding through competitive RFPs to win the work. This also means that you are unlikely to be featured on an analyst's 'Magic Quadrant' or 'Wave', or whatever mechanism they use for rating and comparing similar products. Finally, the product will require a high proportion of consulting/professional services to configure and install.

Multiple buyers

Here is a rule of thumb; if the value delivered by your product has multiple vested interests within the customer then your product will need to be sold Value Created. So you need to consider who is the buyer or are there multiple buyers? If the IT function doesn't have a requirements specification for a product like yours, then it's clear. This is Value Created. If your product needs sign-off from multiple business units or divisions in the organization and the buyer who seems to be most positive needs more senior-level support to purchase, then you are in Value Created territory.

Ben Hood, MD of Fourth Hospitality – a software company catering for the hospitality industry – talks about trying to sell to Gondola, the holding group of Pizza Express:

> *"Yes, we were a bit blind with Gondola. We went all the way through the IMPACT process with Gondola (the holding company) only we did not know it. As a result we had to then go all the way back and do it again with each of the operators and the actual people who ran Pizza Express. We sold it four times. We sold it to the investment house, to the executive board, to the board of Pizza Express and then we sold it to the operators and users. Over one year later we signed the contract and rolled the products out."*

Sales stalled

This happens very often because the customer is trying to buy Value Created and your sales team is working Value Added. Imagine this. You read the sales team reports. There is no shortage of opportunities and there is lots of interest from customers. Except the same names keep appearing on the opportunities list and the forecasted close dates keep moving to the right. Nothing seems to close.[31] Or at least not enough to show a positive trend. Sales guys are starting to get frustrated or spooked. They are running out of their personal contacts so they keep busy with lots of initial meetings, generating customer interest but no second meetings. Customers keep saying "Yes, we like the ideas", but not spending money. Normally this is put down to poor sales people and "You just need some hard-nosed IBM or Oracle salesmen to kick some arse and close the deals." The problem is that when you start really digging into the forecasts, they just dissolve into 'small change'. The sales guys look at the potential revenue, their ability to hit target, and then the cost of the next car or house or boat they want to buy and head back to the safety of an established marketplace where their Value Added sales approach works a treat.

Pilots, no pull-through

This problem is caused by the sales team thinking they are closing a deal when the customer is at the Assessment phase, so it's normally not as stark as no sales. The good salesmen can get their initial customers (their mates) to find enough cash for a pilot from a discretionary budget, but that is where it stops. Do you have a huge number of pilots, or even multiple pilots in a single customer but none of them going anywhere?[32] There is no business case for that 'proper' size deal – deals that are big enough to make operations profitable. This is a most difficult call to make. Maybe you have good, persuasive salesmen. Maybe you just got lucky with a visionary customer or two. But this is not sustainable as the cost of sales for pilots is too high. Eventually the initial excitement and interest in the customer wanes, or the key sponsor moves on and that large profitable follow-on order that everyone predicted and prayed for never comes. Eventually you remove it from the forecast and suddenly the pipeline looks pretty empty.

---

[31] As Douglas Adams said, "I love deadlines. I like the whooshing sound they make as they fly by."
[32] The salesman's nickname is Stelios, because he has as many pilots as Easyjet.

Small incremental sales

Maybe you get beyond a pilot into a small implementation. This is really only splitting hairs. Pilot, small project, Proof of Concept. Just words. Unless you are being positioned for the global roll-out in the customer, then it's all the same thing. High cost of sales with every project in a single customer requires the same sales effort as starting a new customer. This is the same as the 'Pilots, no pull-through' point above except the pain is slightly less intense, but goes on for longer.

Multiple products mask and confuse the sales effort

Now if you are a start-up with one product selling into one market this shouldn't be an issue. You have probably discovered already that you are selling using Value Added and should be Value Created. You can now tear up the company business plan[33] and skip to the next chapter of the book on running a Value Created company.

Most established companies have a range of products. These will typically be sold as Value Added on the salesman's price list, and Value Offered through the same sales team and also on the e-commerce website and followed up by inside sales. If they are constantly innovating then they will have Value Created products, but these will probably be dumped onto the salesman's price list and onto the website.

Multiple products but only one sales team

You only have one sales team, so their skills, motivation, commissions, and hence behavior will be the same for every product. These will not be perfect for every buying culture, nor every product. The products will each have an optimum buying culture with a sales team aligned to it. Wait a minute. Did we just talk about *sales teams*? You mean that there could be more than one sales team? Yes. You already understand the concept. You have field sales – they have cars, phones, egos the size of football pitches, and targets to match. You have inside sales – they have a PC, a phone, a sales target, and

[33] Ideally, not in front of the investors.

60

a fierce ambition to be a field salesman. You could even have a commercial team, who do wacky JV-type deals. So field sales are Value Added. Inside sales are often Value Offered. Commercial sales are Value Captured. We now need to think about a different team who are Value Created.

So we need to consider each proposition vs. buying culture. So what percentage of products, by sales volume or by sales value, is in each area? More importantly, is the relative split where the company wants it to be? Are the sales teams and abilities matched to the proposition spread?

Brand recognition (or aspirations) not aligned with product mix

Do your customers seem confused by you? Operational culture is a huge part of your brand equity. If the sales behavior you are exhibiting is not 'on-brand' then you will be confusing your customers. If all your PR and advertising says that you are innovative (Value Created), but every touch point with the customer is to talk about a product purchase (Value Added or Offered), then this is delivering mixed messages to the customer. If you are a large company, often it is brand strength that gets you into the Board room, not sales capability or buying culture alignment.

Run out of mates and early adopters to sell to

Analyze your customer base and current activity. How many customers are people that you knew before you started your company? Of the rest, how many are early adopters? If the combined total is over 75 percent of your business (use any cut 'n' dice you like), then the signs are not good. Then look at how many of the customers have matured to major purchases or roll-outs, or even progressed beyond early-stage pilots. Are you are stuck in 'Pilots, no pull-through' as discussed earlier?

How interesting is your product?

Now look at your activity. Are you having lots of meetings, loads of interest but no sales? Now you could be cursed by an interesting product as well. Do you have a really cool, clever, neat product which is looking for a problem to solve?

Nick Kingsbury, Private Venture Capitalist of Kingsbury Ventures, has an opinion on this:

> *"Yes. The curse of an interesting product. You almost want a boring product. If it's a really interesting product you end up with people saying does it do this or this, you get people intellectualizing about what it can do as well, that is very difficult territory. I think it can be the death of many start ups, because the customer continues to be interested in the product. The customer says they like your product. The start-up company is thinking they're in Value Added or Value Offered and actually they are over there in the Value Created and they are being used as a free consulting and training service. The worst thing in the world is to have an interesting product. Everyone wants to talk to* **you,** *but no one buys."*

WHY IS VALUE CREATED DIFFICULT?

How can this be so difficult? Before this book was written, companies got launched and products got sold. True. What we are describing is not new. We are simply giving you a framework to understand what has been happening by trial and error, so that you can take out some of the costly time-wasting mistakes.

Why do so many companies not make the move to Value Created when they should? Normally, because they are unaware that there is any other way. Sales is sales is sales. If the founder or CEO is an engineer or inventor, their only direct experience of sales may be as a consumer. In the B2C world, Value Offered always appears to be the norm.

 Most companies are unaware of the buying cultures.

But there are people who do recognize that there is a different way and **still** don't make the change to Value Created. Why not? They probably have a perception that it is too tough, too complex, too risky, and blind faith tells them that good times really must be up ahead. Ignoring the element of blind faith, let's look at the tough, complex, and risky aspects of a Value Created operational culture:

- Tough, because it means getting people to change the way they work, interact, are rewarded, and are motivated.
- Complex, because it will mean making changes across the entire value chain of the business and that means managing politics.
- Risky, because they may not get it right.

So over to blind faith and trust – if we keep doing what we have always done (only a little harder) things might get better.[34]

A VALUE CREATED SALESMAN WORKING IN A VALUE ADDED COMPANY

One of the risks for a Value Added company working without an awareness of the customers' buying cultures is that from its perspective every kind of buying signal means that there is a deal. This is what was happening with our salesman, whom we will call Mike – a Value Created salesman working in a Value Added company:

Mike was selling to the National Health Service (NHS) in the United Kingdom and Mike thought he had a deal for $6 million. In fact, Mike has thought he was about to close a deal for $6 million for the past three quarters. Once Mike had been educated in the concept of buying cultures and the IMPACT process, he

---

[34] The definition of insanity. Doing the same thing today as you did yesterday and expecting the results to be different.

started to think about the behavior of the customer and the kind of people he had been interacting with and none of it added up. He had believed that the customer was at the Case or Transaction phase. This is where a deal will be found if there is one. But the more he looked at IMPACT the more he realized that the customer was displaying none of the behavior expected at the Case or Transaction phases, so Mike took a step back. What did the customer want? It was now clear that it did not yet want solutions or products. But his management was pushing him for sales forecasts. Mike did a deep dive into the customer's world at the Identify phase and started to build an opinion about what was happening with the NHS and not just in its approach to technology. He took this opinion to the CIO and they had a very productive conversation about possibilities which led to a further discovery workshop using consultants from Mike's company. To say that what Mike saw surprised him would be a huge understatement. He was awestruck at the potential that confronted him, but he also saw significant challenges within his own management. Mike's conversation with his management went something like this:

Mike   "Boss, I can see huge potential in this customer."
Boss   "What, more than $6 million?"
Mike   "Much more."
Boss   "How much more?"
Mike   "Five times? Ten times? I can't say for sure at this time."
Boss   "Will it close this quarter?"
Mike   "No."
Boss   "How about this fiscal year?"
Mike   "Unlikely."
Boss   "What about that $6 million you forecast?"

Luckily Mike had a more enlightened Sales Director who saw the same potential that Mike saw and he also recognized that he would have to accept a degree of professional risk if Mike was *to be given a chance to pursue this opportunity. These risks were that for Mike to engage the NHS in a Value Created way he would have to be taken off forecast for that fiscal year. Yet he had a mortgage to pay so would still need to be remunerated in the style he was used to. Next, Mike would need considerable resources in the form of pre-sales and consulting over this period. In the company at that time there were rules which did not allow pre-sales resources to be used on un-forecasted opportunities. Last, how could they measure and report Mike's progress over this year? All of this was reliant on success coming from the relationship and the trust in that relationship that Mike had created with his contacts in the NHS. The Sales Director had the nerve and went with it and in the end Mike closed at $56 million, which at that time was the single largest deal the company had ever done in its history.*

What this example shows very clearly are the factors that stop leaders from making the move to Value Created from deciding to invest in a customer, and getting their heads around forecast management in an extended engagement.

We will leave the last word to the Managing Director of a small company who had hit a $3 million revenue ceiling. He made a half-hearted attempt at building a Value Created division, which was branded The Solutions Group, to break through the ceiling just before the dotcom bubble burst.

"Ladies and Gentlemen

It's with a sad heart that I announce the demise of The Solutions Group. It's too complicated for where we are in our development. We are a young company and need to grow fast, so we are all going to concentrate on bringing in business as fast as possible. Revenue secures our future development and future growth, so from now on it's very simple – SLAM DUNK IT!

> *All sales activities will now report straight to our one sales*
> *manager and he will let you know what he needs in the near*
> *future. We don't need a lot of detail as we are all hardened pro-*
> *fessionals, so let's just get on with it. Close deals."*

Ten months after the MD sent out this email to his staff the business closed.

AND NOW SOME GOOD NEWS

The Value Created buying culture may seem a little strange at first, filled with risk and the unknown. Maybe staying with the current operation is better, even though you recognize that it will ultimately end in tears? Before you give up hope, here's a success story from a company that made a successful transformation. It is not alone.

FLEX Group builds software for major insurance companies, banks, credit unions, and other financial institutions. It is designed to change the way business is done in the inefficient retail financial services sector, which is a multibillion dollar market.

Robert Paterson, Founder and Chairman of Flex, describes how he took his highly innovative product across the chasm in a difficult market. It is such a rollercoaster ride even James Patterson[35] would be proud of it. So here's the story in full:

> *"Founded in 1999 as Eurobenefits, FLEX Group has had a*
> *successful track record of development to date. Its first commer-*
> *cial product known as Mybenefits was rolled out in the UK to a*
> *number of FTSE clients.*

---

[35] Not a relative, but the most successful thriller writer ever: more than $1 billion's worth of books sold (130 million copies worldwide), 16 consecutive American number-one bestsellers, roughly one million books sold every year in Britain alone.

The original idea was very simple. You are a financial advisor and spending all your time setting up employees of large corporates onto company pension schemes. You send your team into the field to try to help people understand their personal finances. When you've educated them, you've got to pull all the information into one place, do a gap analysis between where they are and where they want to get to. You can then decide on the best investment strategy for them.

It's very difficult pulling the data together and it's very expensive sending field sales when you can only penetrate 3% of the company's employees at best. So you have this great unwashed population that has no financial advice and no access. There's a disconnect, yet for insurance companies 90% of their total revenue derives from mass, not the top 3% elite of senior management.

So I figured if you could build a database, do the financial modeling and then show the information in real time, hey presto we could do 20 times more business. That was the basis of the business plan. Then it sort of evolved into something a little bit more substantive, when we raised $6 million and the broker said double the money and double the price because we'd like to back you. They were really supportive and they were really interested in pre IPO stuff. It was a bit of a rollercoaster ride after we raised the first $6 million. I remember doing the AGM in the Barbican Centre and we had about 60 people there and I was giving a speech to all the fund managers in the city. It was the dotcom boom, exciting times. We gave a live demonstration with the computer screen, live demos, pretty cutting edge. It was a pre-empt to raise another $20 million, with $80 million valuation.

We hadn't finished the product but we had some sales guys and there were a whole range of customers. Of course, having lined up customers is very different from getting a customer to sign up. We did win some fairly major customers, but we weren't entirely convinced at the end whether it was sustainable because the perception and the reality are very different.

What we kind of discovered was that we had the leading edge technology, this is seriously advanced kit, very avant-garde. In reality we were ahead of our time. We got the early adopters. We were at least 2 if not 3 years ahead of the market and this was both good and bad. The good part of it was that we had something that was cutting edge. The first fully automated employee benefit system in the UK. The bad thing was that we discovered the Value Created sales cycle could be long and of course during 2000 we had the dotcom crash. But even late in 2000 we had investment backers flying over from the States saying we want to float you for $500 million – seriously mad I know. They thought it was just the most brilliant thing.

We were in the technology innovation center at Accenture for two years as best of breed in Europe. Particularly after 9/11 it all slowed right down and it was very difficult to get anyone to actually make a commitment or decision when you've got new technology. So now the sales cycle was at least 12 months which was a problem.

We had sales people who were probably capable of dealing at SME level but not capable of dealing at the enterprise Board level. It was a problem and in retrospect we should not have had that sales team but 1 or 2 really top guys instead. A smaller team going in as a strategic sale to the tier 1 customer as opposed to focusing on the SMEs.

Investment froze up anyway at that point. I think everyone believed in the model, believed it was a really smart idea but nobody really knew what the sales cycle was going to be. And of course the sales cycles were getting longer and longer and then it didn't help not being entirely sure about your business model. So you are now thinking, if it takes 12 months to make a sale to a FTSE 100, you have to have a hell of a lot of cash in the bank to finance that. We really needed to raise 2 or 3 times more capital than we had to allow us to ride the whole thing out.

It was around this time I was joined by Simon Reeve as CEO. *Simon played a pivotal role helping me manage and re-shape the business as we realized we urgently needed to change our business strategy to focus on licensing to insurance companies with millions of customers. At the end of the day that was the conclusion we came to, that there's a secondary opportunity which was to license the systems to the insurance companies themselves. They've got millions of customers and our software is all about joining the product provider, the customer and the broker. It's a hub. The insurance company pays a fortune in commission for the broker to sell a product but the insurer has no idea which product the guy has sold as he's got no relationship. The broker can only see the 3%, so why don't we just license this to the insurance companies?*

We changed the strategy, and I said we need to partner, probably with a life company with 5 million customers. We had 5 companies lined up. We'd already done a proposal for Aegon to license the product. I flew up to Scotland on Friday and I phoned up the FD at Aegon who I'd known a long time, and I just said I'm in Scotland and I'm seeing five potential companies up here. Anyway, I walked into his office in Edinburgh and he said straight away "You've done a proposal for us, and we don't want to invest in you, we'd actually like to buy you." I said "That's an interesting idea, will think about it." Actually, the deal was done. I didn't say we were short of cash. We weren't – we were very short of cash. I said "You need to put £150,000 in the bank by Wednesday otherwise I'll go off and see the others I've lined up. That's a commitment fee to do the deal, non refundable." We shook hands on it and £75,000 was in by Wednesday, the rest by Friday. I took the lunchtime plane back. Later that month we cut the final deal.

It's now the leading distribution platform for Aegon in the UK. They have clients like Schweppes and the BBC as users of the system. It's a brilliant product, it's fantastic, it's the number one in the UK.

It was a killer product, one of the very few survivors of the period and it was ahead of its time. I thought it was going to make a fortune – off the Richter scale. I thought everyone is going to recognize it, and of course it didn't happen as planned.
But we delivered the result we all dreamed of."

Do you still have the stomach for a Value Created operational culture? If so, then read on Macduff . . .[36]

---

[36] Actually the question is: Do you really have a choice? And also, do you know what the real Shakespeare quotation is?

CHAPTER 5

The magic of a Value Created company

THE PERFECT STORM

A salesman who really understands the Value Created engagement can drive significantly higher value engagements with greater margin. But timing is critical, as is that initial entry point.[37]

Richard Beasley, Sales Director at BT Global Services, describes a perfect Value Created sales engagement. This is what it's like when it all comes together:

> *"I remember a really good example from when I was at Equant (now Orange Business Services). Actually the credit goes to the sales guy for originally picking up an article in the press about the merger between the two organizations Colep and CCL, both*

---

[37] "You don't get a second chance to create a first impression" could never be truer than here.

manufacturers of metal and plastic packaging. We felt that the merger of these two organizations, one predominantly US based, the other European, was an opportunity since clearly there was going to be significant change in the new organization. This sales guy had the confidence to go to the top. He quickly engaged with the CIO and was able to demonstrate that Equant had an understanding of their particular business situation. It turned out the two companies were integrating and the CIO's remit was to provide an IT infrastructure to support the globalization of the business through a single global brand. Managing the business across a number of continents required the implementation of an ERP system, which in turn meant they needed a secure and highly available networking infrastructure. By demonstrating our value to their business in achieving these goals we were able to keep the discussion just with Equant, which in turn the customer benefited from a fast tracked implementation and savings on a costly RFP process. We did a main board presentation which resulted in a services contract covering not just their global networking infrastructure, security and mobile worker requirements, but also their voice services with plans to extend services to their local area networks and over time converge all ICT services onto a single IP based architecture.

If it hadn't been for the confidence of going in at that high level talking about our opinion on how we could manage their merger risks and the business benefits we could bring, it would have been completely different. At best we would end up responding to an RFP that came from the organization and for a deal would have been worth about a quarter of what we actually won and at a lot lower margin.

The ease and simplicity was surprising. The initial engagement was done within the sales team itself. It was sales account manager and myself looking through the merger report, pulling together some information from the internet and between us *coming up with an opinion that the sales guy was going to present to the CIO when he called him up. For me the two key elements of Value Creation are first you can create the interest with the client but then second you have to back it up with some substance. If you don't do that then you are very quickly going to lose the confidence of the client and your dialogue will just fizzle out.*

From the internal perspective we're all competing for resource. We needed technical resource to design a solution, but we were able to quantify the opportunity in terms of value, our USP, who the key decision makers were and the politics. I was one of a number of sector managers. The Value Created engagement helped me ensure I could get the right resources on the opportunities that my team was working on. It allowed me to put together a well reasoned case of why we thought this opportunity was a good one to follow."

THE CASE FOR CHANGE

Some of you may have already spotted that alignment to the customer's buying culture is pretty fundamental to corporate strategy.[38] If you are a start-up it is **THE** critical decision, because no sales equals death or a VC-funded slow death – but death nevertheless.

Craig Johnson, Chairman of the Venture Law Group, likes to say

"The leading cause of failure of startups is death, and death happens when you run out of money. As long as you have money, you're still in the game."

[38] Unless, of course, you have randomly opened the book up at this page and started reading.

If you are an established company and committed to innovate, then alignment to the customer's buying culture is critical to how you organize the company. If you are not interested in innovation it will help you decide which products to offload.

A critical look at your sales strategy for certain products may show that you should consider moving to a Value Created operational culture.

 The most critical strategic decision is how to align to the customer's buying culture.

We are going to look at the Value Created operational culture from a number of different perspectives. We are going to look through the eyes of a range of companies in different industries, with different levels of maturity and different sizes. Their insights are invaluable as they are real and tangible and come with the scars of experience. We'll look at each area along the Value Chain in turn and then the support functions; i.e. Management, R&D, Marketing, Sales, Delivery, and then Support (HR, IT, and Finance).

MANAGEMENT

Executive leadership

Based on your answer to the next question, you may stop reading right here.

Do you have the nerve to transition to a Value Created operational culture?

If there is any sign of doubt from the leadership then nobody will dare make the necessary changes. If you've got the nerve then what do you need to do next?

Your role as a leader is to have the nerve. To make the tough decisions. To lead with conviction.

Nick Watson, VP Europe at Cisco Systems, suggests that the first step is to challenge, educate, and engage the entire business on value creation:

> *"I think you actually need to take the entire company and cause it to think about value and Value Creation. I don't think it's fair or even workable to say that this is the job just solely of one department. You might indeed say that Value Creation is the marketing department's role but you can't really just do this in one area of the company. You have to go right across the company."*

So, what skills does the leader need for this company at this stage of its evolution? Matthew Mead, Partner at 3i Venture Capital, offers some insight into why companies seem to stall or plateau at $6 million to $10 million annual revenue:

> *"You also get a lot of people who are able to grow a company to the $6 million to $10 million revenue level. Some of them are founders who built the company, some of them aren't. Maybe they've done several VC backed CEO roles and they're probably always looking for the company that might break through. But there probably aren't that many that do. I think the first barrier is between $6 million to $10 million. What we often see is companies get to this with 50/60 people, 12 guys in sales, 20 guys in R&D, and they can't grow any further. I can think of three or four companies that I worked with in this situation. Every year we say we will break through and don't."*

Business model

Bizarrely, the margins in the Value Created world are very tight. Not because of competitive price wars or even competitive tendering. What causes the problems are the long sales cycles. Whilst the 'pre-sales' consulting is paid, it is still 'pre-sales' and needs to be completed before the larger, more profitable product sale.

"Are we a consulting firm or a product company?" is a constant question inside the company and by the investors.[39] Strangely, the customers are very clear that you are a product company and don't seem to get nearly so confused. They simply want what they want. If you mirror their buying culture with your operational culture it all becomes a whole lot simpler.

However, you will be running a complex organization. It has R&D, Marketing, Pre-sales, Direct Sales, Software Hosting, Professional Services, and Support, all of which need to mesh together to give a seamless customer experience. You could run a far simpler business – such as a Value Offered commodity business – but this is a tough dog-eat-dog environment. Or you could be running a Value Added business, but unless you are the 500lb gorilla you will always be fighting for the scraps. The reason for undergoing the pain and anguish of running a highly effective Value Created company is that YOU become the gorilla when your market changes from Value Created to Value Added. And that is when the money starts pouring in – provided you spot that the market has changed and you change your operational culture to Value Added.

Key Performance Indicators and metrics

Value Created cannot be driven quickly and easily using a standard CRM solution. These are designed for the traditional Value Added or Value Offered markets, with simple, shorter sales cycles – which also means that

---

[39] With the natural concerns about valuation of the company.

it is less easy to drag out the key metrics. The metrics for Value Created focus as much on growth as on margin improvement or salesman productivity. As you are looking at longer sales cycles, you need to consider leading vs. lagging indicators. For a fuller description of the differences between leading and lagging, go to the Appendix.

Some of the metrics may look like the following:

- Revenue growth by customer vs. cost of sales, where revenue is product + professional services.
- Number of sector marketing initiatives which make it to Assessment phase per customer.
- How many sales and professional services staff have a security pass for their customer (so they can roam freely).
- Percentage of open opportunities closed on forecast close date.
- Backlog, which is the amount of Purchase Order cover for professional services and software hosting which is still to be delivered.

Companies within companies

Multiple products means multiple buying cultures, which means multiple operational cultures. But cultures clash. None more so than Value Captured and Value Created. Value Added and Value Offered seem to co-exist happily. So, one approach is to spin off the highly innovative divisions. Put them in a separate location. Samantha Hinton bought 81G out from the parent company and started again:

"Having identified a gap in the market, 81G was born as a simple yet effective concept of selling IT managed services to SMB's (Small and Medium sized Businesses). Taking the idea to the investment board of PIMS, an established and successful company, the idea received enthusiastic approval. Major investment

was given and 81G was established as a sub division of PIMS. It was set up as a mini corporate environment with a CEO, COO, CTO, a New Business Manager, sales staff, a PR agency and a marketing manager, three engineers and a customer care officer. Everything was set to handle what was assumed to be an immediate influx of business.

But six months later, 81G was not generating any of its own leads and had not even garnered a sale. It was, in fact, hemorrhaging money and only remained buoyant thanks to the support of its parent company. Fundamentally, I believe it all came down to the fact that 81G was hamstrung by its governance and operating methods, being too similar to its parent and that of a corporate – the two just didn't marry.

So, given an opportunity to become independent, two of the executive management team took the business on in February 2007, setting it up as a pseudo company away from the gazing eyes of its parent. Firstly, we streamlined the entire business, created a different business strategy, productizing and re-modelling it. By July 2007 we had broken even."

Mike Harris was founder of First Direct and Egg, two companies that shook up the UK consumer financial services industry by putting the customer first. Whilst CEO of Prudential's banking division, in 1998 Harris launched a mass-market, customer-focused, internet-enabled bank, called Egg. It was a bold move for Prudential – a huge, conservative-minded corporation. In pure marketing terms Egg was an instant success. It had met its 5-year target for customer acquisition within just 6 months. It wasn't profitable, but in those frothy internet times the analysts valued it at \$9bn. So in 2000, with the stockmarket white hot, a flotation was planned to raise credibility and more cash for expansion. But there was another reason. There were conflicting priorities between the Prudential board and the entrepreneurial Egg team. It wasn't 'fractious' but it was rapidly becoming clear, in the words of Sir Peter Davies, Prudential board member and an ally of Harris, that "Prudential would eventually kill Egg". So the flotation would allow Egg to be spun off to protect it, as the 'parental control' of Prudential was starting to exasperate the founders of Egg. "There was some interference", Harris recalls. "I spent a lot of time stopping that interference getting in the way, and ultimately that interference kills. It just keeps coming at you . . ." Prudential finally sold Egg to Citigroup for just over $1bn, a loss of $500m. At the time the Prudential CEO argued that the sale maximized shareholder value. But the charge of 'parental interference' maybe had an influence. As Harris remembers, "You can protect against corporate policy for so long, but in the end it's: Why are they different? Why are they paying everyone differently? Why don't they use the same rules and systems we're using? Why aren't they selling our products? Why are they so independent?"

R&D

The early stage Proof of Concept project is as much consulting as it is product. The aim is to sell the product, but in the early stages the product is a barrier. The evangelist wants to use it. Buying consulting is easy. Buying a product is hard. IT and procurement want to get involved. Is it the cheapest? What infrastructure does it commit us to for the next 5 years? What warranty and support costs are there? You need to sidestep these issues. The simplest way is to rent it if it is a product, or host it (Software as a Service) if it is software.

Remember, these customers are early adopters. They don't need 100 percent finished product. 70 percent will do, provided they are confident that it will be 100 percent at some stage. Until then they will lobby the supplier for their pet changes to be released next. That means, to be responsive the R&D organization needs to be geared up to deliver in rapid release cycles. The risk is that with too many customers with competing demands, eventually you will get stretched too thin.

Adrian King, Nimbus COO, describes the pressure to deliver product enhancements to an increasing client base from the perspective of a rapidly growing software company:

> *"When we were small and had only 2 or 3 strategic customers we could support them and commit to working with them to develop the complete product. As we have expanded, we have far more Fortune 1000 customers, with more propositions, across more geographies than ever before. And it's putting massive tension into R&D and marketing. R&D because every client wants the product completed for their specific need. Marketing because they are trying to 'complete' the product for each proposition. Prioritization is key, but against what criterion? Lifetime value? Loudest salesman? Fastest route to revenue? One way to ease the pain is to start to focus on a couple of key propositions, as suggested in Crossing the Chasm.*
>
> *For Nimbus the focus is SAP implementations, as our product Control 2007 can drive up end-user adoption of new SAP implementations, by massively de-risking the early blueprinting phase for customers and the Systems Implementers, and then using that blueprint (process content) for user testing, training and ongoing operation."*

Iterative product development is a good approach for a Value Created operational culture. There's no point saying to sales people in a vacuum, "What should we make next?" It is better to engage them early by saying, "We're thinking of making something. How will it be accepted by the competition"? "It provides a straw man for feedback for customer user groups, and allows the salesmen to engage customers strategically."

MARKETING

Value Created marketing is much, much more than sales support. The marketing team needs to educate a customer to develop the market, but unless you have the marketing budget of a major consumer brand or Microsoft, then forget it. You need to resort to guerrilla marketing. Techniques that work are publishing a book about the principles,[40] which makes it easier to be invited to speak as the guru or thought-leader at conferences, running seminars and breakfast briefings on specific issues, and writing White Papers. Presentations should be educative rather than product-oriented or a sales pitch.[41]

A VP Marketing of a major global telco describes how developing a partnership with the customer can be viewed very cynically. But done well, with the correct intentions, it is hugely powerful:

> *"I think the interesting thing is that when you look at a lot of what are deemed as strategic engagement or partnership type interactions with customers. Everybody gets very cynical and very quickly points to examples of where partnerships haven't worked. So the phrase of partnership is extremely devalued. I challenge sales teams by asking them how they are going to establish this intimate relationship with their customer. How are they going to be seen as valuable extensions to the work that their customers do for their end users. This is a deeper understanding of what the wider customer business is trying to achieve and allows a sales person to have a strategic discussion with senior people. We have a number of good examples of where a Value Created engagement has produced intimate relationships and marketing has a key role to play here."*

Martin Brown, Senior Director, Enterprise Sales at Symantec talks about his approach to joint sales and marketing in a Value Created sale:

> *"As far as industry marketing goes, we have a unified sales and marketing team. They should be looking at the aspects of value*

---

[40] About the principles behind the product. Not the product explicitly, or this is seen as marketing material and not thought-leadership.
[41] The pen (and flipchart) are mightier than 20 MS PowerPoint slides.

creation in the geographies that we want to attack together. Identifying industry trends or business drivers and how we approach them from both a marketing and sales perspective is critical. Industry marketing can be CIO round-tables, it can be more research and events. So my industry sales directors are responsible for the development of the industry marketing plans for their sectors. They have direct input and personal sign-off on the industry marketing plans."

SALES

 In a Value Created company you will spend much more time with people who will never buy from you.

Customer relationship

Andy Berry, GM of Fuji Xerox Global Services, explains how they have used IMPACT to help make better management decisions, and really drive the sales process:

"We're quite clear on our use of the IMPACT process and the different operational cultures to drive the sales engagements. Previously, we believed [we] had a 'one size fits all' marketing and sales management process. We used to assume that we were engaging the customer at Identify and we would try and get our sales force to go through Mentor, Position and Assessment on every single deal. Now, what the operational culture model has given us is the ability to acknowledge that quite often we are

actually engaging with the customer at Case and this is [a] Value Added deal. We have also recognized that frequently the customer has got to Case having missed out many of the risk analysis steps within the earlier phases which are very important to make a sound business decision. Sometimes it's so important that we need to help the customers go back and mend holes in their own internal processes. When that happens you have the added benefit of getting closer to them and becoming a trusted advisor. This protects our customer relationship, qualifies our risk investment and protects us from any competition."

A critical part of this is assessing which IMPACT phase the customer is in. Then, you have to mirror their behavior. It is when you get out of sync, normally ahead of the customer, that your forecasting of sales closes goes wrong. Opportunities seem to keep slipping. As Andy Berry explains, understanding the IMPACT process makes the sales cycle more transparent:

"It has really helped to streamline a lot of our business decision making across all operational cultures. The sales cycles aren't necessarily a lot harder. But now when we are in a really complex sales cycle, as a management team we consciously understand what we are doing and all think and discuss the subject in the same 'language'. Marketing, sales, finance, professional services and operations all share a common understanding. Now, we all know which phase our customer is at, what we should be doing at that phase and where we are going next."

Customer engagement

This is about capturing the customer's imagination with something that is insightful and relevant. Something about their business that they have missed or not appreciated. But it is offered up **not** as bait which will hook them, or with strings attached. It is offered with no expectation of work or any relationship, whilst clearly there is a hope on the supplier side that this will develop. The VP Marketing of a major global telco describes how introducing two CIOs, who were both facing the same challenges implementing SAP, has forged a strong relationship with both:

> *"We know the CIO and CFO of a large packaging manufacturer very well. They are a big client of ours. They have bought into our company in a big way. Likewise we know the CIO of a large food production group. When I was meeting with him, he was talking to me about the use of the single instance of SAP across their operation, the CIO of this packaging manufacturer had gone through [a] similar exercise, and that Gartner had done a fantastic report for him. We brought the two of them together. Our company participated in the meeting but really the interaction was between the two CIOs and they really derived immense value from the conversation. What we got out of that was phenomenal. We understood a lot more about what the Packaging Company was doing in other parts of their interactions with [the] supplier and the way their business operated. This has opened up a completely different area for us to interact with them."*

These relationships with customers are deep and meaningful when there is no expectation of reward. This is something that Guy Kawasaki, author of *The Art of the Start*,[42] calls "being a mensch". A mensch is a Yiddish term and is described as: Someone to admire and emulate, someone of noble character. The key to being 'a real mensch' is nothing less than character, rectitude, dignity, a sense of what is right, responsible, decorous.

---

[42] A summary of the book is in the Appendix.

Here are four ideas from Guy Kawasaki to become a mensch:

- *Help people who cannot help you.* A mensch helps people who cannot ever return the favor. He doesn't care if the recipient is rich, famous, or powerful. This doesn't mean that you shouldn't help rich, famous, or powerful people (indeed, they may need the most help), but you shouldn't help only rich, famous, and powerful people.
- *Help without the expectation of return.* A mensch helps people without the expectation of return – at least in this life. What's the payoff? Not that there has to be a payoff, but the payoff is the pure satisfaction of helping others. Nothing more, nothing less.
- *Help many people.* Menschdom is a numbers game: you should help many people, so you don't hide your generosity under a bushel. Of course, not even a mensch can help everyone. To try to do so would mean failing to help anyone.
- *Do the right thing the right way.* A mensch always does the right thing the right way. He would never take an attitude like, "We're not as bad as Enron." There is a bright, clear line between right and wrong, and a mensch never crosses that line.

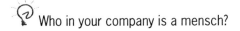 Who in your company is a mensch?

Sounds a little OTT? In the world of big business, quarterly earnings targets, and tough competition, Jeremy Greaves, VP Communications and PR for EADS, talks about the importance of developing a close customer relationship, and the time that this takes to grow. Combine this with the examples of how Value Created engagements started, and it doesn't sound so different from Guy Kawasaki's 'menschdom':

"Developing an intimate customer relationship is not something that can just be bought by taking your customer to Wimbledon,

a Formula 1 Grand Prix or a football game. Corporate hospitality, or corporate hostility as it is sometimes known as, is just an excuse to start a 'conversation of possibilities'. It should never be seen as a transaction or a one-off. If you really want to get close to the customer then you need to build trust and credibility over time. But more importantly it is how well you really understand the customer's business. From that understanding you are able to support the customer which gives them a tangible benefit, a real business impact. That is what builds a strong and long-lasting relationship – but it takes time and patience."

Rushing through IMPACT to get to T

Sales guys can see and virtually taste the order.[43] The mentor reckons that this should be pretty easy and is impatient, so wants to get to T (Transaction) as much as the salesman. Maybe he sees this as his big chance to make a name for himself. But it seems to be stalling at the Assessment stage. Whilst it seems counterintuitive, don't keep pushing but look at the following:

- Is there still the executive sponsorship, or have some of the players left or changed?
- Is the evidence still valid or has the business changed?

If you don't have sponsorship AND valid evidence, then GO BACK to the Position stage and start again. This may seem painful, but it will be faster, cheaper, and easier than trying to force through the next stage, because without the sponsorship and evidence you will NEVER get a PO.

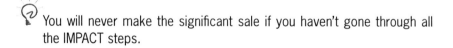 You will never make the significant sale if you haven't gone through all the IMPACT steps.

---

[43] Actually they can see the commission.

Adrian King, COO of Nimbus, tells the story of a client who some 2 years later, has still not raised the PO:

> "*We were young and naïve. We hadn't heard of buying cultures. All we knew was that we had a great product and customers loved it. We had worked really hard to open up a major UK utility. We had supported them on their (paid) pilots. The pilots had been seen as a great success across the business. So together with our internal sponsor, we agreed that we should propose a national rollout. Our proposal was submitted to the Board and after several iterations it was accepted. A contract was drawn up and after long and painful negotiations with procurement it was agreed with a software license value of $1m. It was signed by all 13 signatories. Result – but no PO. We were promised a PO, so we waited patiently, then less patiently, and then started chasing. Eventually we found out that the FD, who was at the Board meeting and a signatory on the contract had vetoed the PO, as he was able to do. Two years after signing of the contract we still haven't received a PO. But we have done more than $1m of revenue supporting them through the IMPACT process – properly this time. Now they understand the value of the product and the software license value will be far more than the original $1m.*"

The Value Created salesman

A very successful Value Created salesman who works for a major software supplier was tasked with breaking into the BBC. He approached it in a Value Created way, textbook fashion. He used his marketing and consulting resources to deep-dive the world of the BBC, particularly its future, and from this work he came up with an opinion about some future risks that the COO of the BBC would probably be unaware of. He crafted a succinct and attention-grabbing letter which he then asked his European VP to sign and send. The result was an executive engagement at levels not normally known in his company. He has used this executive engagement to establish new revenue streams and mentors to manage them. You might have a picture in your mind of some silver-haired, wise, and wily salesman with 20 years' experience at Oracle or IBM but you'd be wrong, this salesman is just 27 years old.[44]

Years of sales experience is irrelevant. It is years of *relevant* sales experience that counts.

We have had many debates about what makes a Value Created salesman, is it nature or nurture or a bit of both? If so, what is the balance? Some are actually born this way and it is all they know. These people can find life in anything but a Value Created company quite hard because nobody understands them. When they are successful they are called lucky because they have become a threat to their sales manager. So nature vs. nurture:

Nature is energy, inquisitiveness, intellectual bandwith, openness to change, willingness to help irrespective of who gets the credit, and desire to improve.

Nurture is the training, exposure to more open thinking, presenting without a PowerPoint deck, open easy networking, ongoing reviews, coaching, and support. It is providing easy access to industry trend materials. If you are in a large organization, you can start to explore these things in real-life format in CIO round-tables, at dinners, and events.

---

[44] If you are a recruitment consultant you have probably thrown this book in the bin at this point.

Martin O'Byrne, VP Strategy at Atos Origin, explains 'RSVP' as the emotional foundation for Value Created salesmen, where RSVP = Resolute, Straightforward, Vibrant, and Personal:

- "**Resolute** means determined, consistent and driving with focus. I want to win for me (Atos Origin) and for you (the customer).
- **Straightforward** means direct open honest communication. Simple rather than convoluted and incomprehensible. Simple rather than simplistic because I portray the essence and stay on point. Find the simple/elegant solution in a complex world.
- **Vibrant** means that you will feel my passion and energy and believe that that is what Atos Origin is about and that is what it will feel like working with us.
- **Personal** means personal to you (the individual customer I am dealing with and the benefit/value of the outcomes) as well as the wider client organization but also recognizing that I (Atos Origin) need to win as well."

A good way to understand the Value Created salesman is to compare him to his nearest neighbor, the Value Added salesman, against a whole range of attributes:

Commission plans and incentives

How you incentivize salesmen will always be a thorny issue. We all know that people act as they are measured. Salesmen are entirely driven by their compensation package. Change the package and you will be staggered by how quickly behaviors change.[45]

---

[45] If only this were true about other changes you want them to make: compliance to process, using the new CRM solution correctly, putting the toilet seat down, etc.

	VALUE ADDED	VALUE CREATED
What they say	"Let me demo you the product. It's awesome"	"Let's discuss what you are trying to achieve. Do you have a pen/whiteboard?"
Every meeting	. . . is a planned step towards a PO	. . . is a 'conversation of possibilities'
Previous track record	Top performing salesman	Partner or senior-level consultant
Sales & delivery approach	Sell, collect commission, and move on	Work with the customer to deliver results
Commissioned	OTE on product gross margin	On total project value
Most valuable attributes	Hungry, driven, and materialistic	Trusted, patient, and persistent
Greatest achievement	Exceeded OTE last 20 quarters (i.e., 5 years) running	Sitting on the Board or Project Steering Committee of his main customer
How customer sees them	A supplier selling their product	Trusted advisor with a supporting product
Where do they hang out	Company reception waiting for Procurement and IT Managers	Executive Suite and business sponsor's office
How to get a deal in quicker	Drop their trousers! Discount, discount, discount	Political leverage. Discounts don't work. Support and coaching for project manager might help
Title on business card	VP Sales	Nothing very often, or perhaps Partner

Nick Watson, VP Europe at Cisco Systems, has this perspective:

> *"Sales get this quite quickly. They do understand. But Value Creation is not the easiest thing to do. In many cases you will be asking somebody to stop doing something that might make them money in the short term and to actually think bigger to achieve more in the longer term. But if I am a salesman and my compensation plan is driven off quarterly sales quota and doesn't match the Value Creation strategy then that isn't going to work. The number one challenge is the alignment of compensation, pay plans and reward structures towards Value Creation."*

One of the most difficult issues connected to Value Created salesmen and incentives is the subject of capping sales commissions. Personally we don't quite understand the logic other than senior management jealousy. If the guy is selling twice what he should, that 'second million' is pretty profitable for the company as is the third, fourth, and fifth, so why not pay him for it and drive some explosive growth? Spend time and energy getting the commission right and driving the correct behaviors rather than worrying about how much your top salesman makes.

Sales operations

So in a Value Created environment how do you plan and then have confidence that you can hit your revenue targets? The only way is to have a large number of potential projects all running in parallel. Then in any given month or quarter, enough opportunities close to ensure the growth of the company. Discounting to encourage a purchase in a specific quarter does not work. Often the product purchase is dependent on the professional services and that relies on the availability of the customer team. So the approach is to accept that out of the possible 50 opportunities, 15 will close in a particular month. That doesn't mean that you can't manage your pipeline. The disciplines of tracking an opportunity and supporting the customer remain important. The critical difference is that there is little you can do to force a purchase to meet your quotas.

Adrian King, COO of Nimbus, talks about the challenge of forecasting with a Value Created operational culture:

> "*When we were going through the implications of Value Created sales engagements we realized that it affected all the operational areas of the business not just sales. We found we had opportunities emerging (especially for services) at each phase – i.e. the client was asking us to support them at each phase of the IMPACT lifecycle. And each opportunity then had its own forecast life cycle.*
>
> *I believe that you should not focus on forecasting pipeline but managing the engagement that you have with the client. The point is you are reporting on actuals – e.g. what phase you are at with each client. The next month forecast and the closed this month are still important, in fact vital for cash management, but pipeline forecasting gets replaced by the reporting on the engagement phase. The issue is trying to forecast pipeline which 6 months out is normally not worth anything from a sales management point of view. It's sometimes misleading and can actually be dangerous. You could get complacent as your pipeline 6–12 months out looks strong, but the shape, size and a start date of the opportunity could easily change as it gets closer. The message is that if you manage, and monitor the engagement through the buying lifecycle the revenue will follow as a consequence.*"

Partner ecosystem

The traditional channels such as VARs will not work for you. The name says everything – Value Added Resellers. The best third parties to help you sell are niche consulting firms who can sell their services to support the education of your customers. Finding those that are genuinely 'on message' will be difficult. Often the smaller firms are best, where you can really engage with their CEO or Managing Director.[46] But remember that

---

[46] As you were told at school, "pick on someone your own size".

they have a different agenda from you. They want to sell man-days, not product. So you will need to support them with your direct sales force. But the salesmen need to be very sensitive to the needs of the consulting firm. Go in heavy-handed pushing product and they will never be invited back. They should morph so that they look and feel like part of the consulting firm's own team.

Martin Brown, Senior Director, Enterprise Sales at Symantec reflects on how the Alliance Managers he led at Sun Microsystems were able to function in a Value Created way:

"Well, first and most obvious was because they'd been recruited as being very high-performing end user sales people. So they had a track record of high-value, large deals for major corporates before they became Alliances Managers. There were very few members of the team who had only known a Value Added world. I think that's why when you marry an understanding of high-value end sales cycles and an appreciation of the contribution that good alliances can make, then the Value Created approach becomes obvious. And for us that was the key element of competitive advantage."

The extended sales force

The first thing to realize is that in the Value Created world you will be focusing on fewer customers, so managing fewer opportunities. But each opportunity will be far bigger and strategically more important for the customer – in the long term.

But you don't have to do it on your own. There is an effective sales force that you can tap into – the evangelists in your customers. These are the visionary, early adopters. You need to support them, educate them, and nurture them. They will take you around the organization. If your product is as good as you claim, they should get promoted or move to another company and introduce you there. Your job is to make evangelists look great. They are putting their reputations and jobs on the line. They need to ensure that they are not considered to be your sales team inside the customer, and therefore lose their credibility. Don't be surprised if they want to work for you.

At times they become too evangelical and are seen to have become salesmen for the product of the company. You need to watch for this and be able to 'change evangelist' within the organization. As you change from phase to phase in the IMPACT process, you may need to find an evangelist with different attributes. Early on in Identify, Mentor, and Position, they need to be visionary, open-minded, and well-connected. As you enter the Assessment and Case phases you need a 'completer-finisher', who can get stuff done. Once you are into Transaction, then it's out of their hands.

 An evangelist normally has no more than 2 years evangelizing a product within a company before they run out of steam or lose credibility.

DELIVERY

By Delivery we mean pre-sales and professional services. In the Value Created world, there is limited unpaid pre-sales. The customer will pay for the early work, so pre-sales blurs into professional services. In the same way that in some cases the account manager morphs into a consultant and is paid to work with the customer. This chameleon-like ability to "be selling one minute to the customer and being paid for their time the next minute" is the highest level that a Value Created salesman can reach.

So, in the Value Added world, all work prior to the award of a contract is considered free pre-sales. In the Value Created world there may be a number of paid consulting projects to help the customer navigate through the Position, Assessment, and Case phases.

Consultants are the best salesmen. Because they gain the trust of the customer, empathize with them, and virtually 'go-native', the consultant's advice is sought after. The consultant is the eyes and ears for the salesman. It is perfectly normal for the consultant to be dragged away by the mentor or sponsor, off the project work they were engaged in, to talk to other areas of business, do demos, or give advice.

SUPPORT

HR/recruitment

Recruiting a team to make Value Created sales is not straightforward – particularly the sales guys. You can see they are a curious mix of strategy consultant, trainer, and salesman. You will probably find that the best recruits were consultants in a previous life who could sell, rather than Value Added salesmen with a consultative style. The sales team is the most expensive resource in a Value Created company – to hire, to pay, to support, and to fire. It is critical that you get as few PURE[47] candidates as possible. Firstly the sales cycle in Value Created is long, so it takes a while – 6 months or more – to establish if the salesman is performing. And it could be longer if they turn up with a black book listing a few mates who can make early purchases which masks their lack of long-term potential. So not only is there the cost of recruiting them, firing them, and replacing them, but there is the lost opportunity cost. In the Value Created world, time is the most expensive resource. You need to establish your company as the gorilla before the market matures to Value Added. You cannot afford to waste time. So HR has a critical role to play. They really need to understand the Value Created model, so that the sales, pre-sales, and consultants you hire are a perfect fit. And as these are a scarce

---

[47] Previously Unrecognized Recruiting Error.

resource, they will need to look at a huge number of candidates and be patient, rather than drop their standards to fill vacancies.[48]

One approach which works well, but is often misunderstood, is working with a retained recruitment company. They will become an extended part of the recruitment team. You spend time educating them and they can do the frog-kissing (see footnote 48). Why retained rather than on a commission basis? Bizarrely, most recruitment companies are commissioned candidate by candidate, because that is what customers seem to want. But this drives the wrong behavior. And it is counterproductive in a market of scarce resources, where poor recruiting decisions really punish you.

Nick Daniels, founder of DanielsReeve, a recruitment agency, explains how he struggles to get most customers to understand why paying him a retainer to be the exclusive recruiter is a good idea for both him and the customer. But being paid by retainer means he is completely in sync with his customer's objectives:

> *"If you are paid for each candidate placed, then it's a one-off transaction. The higher the salary you can get for the candidate the higher the commission. The faster you can find a candidate that "just" meets the criteria, the quicker you get your commission and can move onto the next vacancy in the next client. Sales incentives drive behavior and it forces me to work for the candidate and multiple clients; Value Offered. But this behavior is completely misaligned with client's objectives. If I'm paid by a monthly retainer then I'm on the client's side. An extension of their recruitment department or for small companies I am their recruitment department. It makes business sense for me to really understand their needs, and suggest better approaches as I share*

---

[48] They will need to kiss a lot of frogs to find the princes.

in their success; Value Created. And I'm now incentivized to find and place only the perfect candidates, sell the benefits of the client's company to them and negotiate their salary down."

IT hosting/loan/rental

You will need to find ways to support your mentor and accelerate use of your product, whilst at the same time de-risking it for them. If you have a physical product then that may mean short-term loans or renting the product. This is another cost which needs to be factored into the business model.

If you have a software product the ability to 'lend' the software on an extended trial basis is unlimited. There is no cost of manufacture to worry about. However, that software needs to run on a computer somewhere. That normally means involving the customer's IT department. And that is a BAD thing. They are normally early majority and are used to buying in a Value Added or Value Offered manner. They will stop the project dead in the water, possibly for months. So an alternative approach is to provide your software as a hosted service (SaaS). Your customer can rent it on a monthly or quarterly basis. It is paid for from an operational budget rather than capital expenditure, which is appealing to your mentor who is trying to keep it 'under the corporate radar'.

However, a word of warning. Your mentor would probably like to keep it away from his corporate IT department for ever because it is hassle he does not need. They will ask for business cases, have technical questions, and probably want to purchase an alternative product. But before your product can be rolled out to a wider community – i.e., the BIG sale – it will need IT's blessing and support. So you will need to coach your mentor about the right time to engage IT and the right way to do it, and then force him to do it.[49]

---

[49] Like going to the dentist. You know it's a good idea in the long term, but the thought of the short-term pain stops you.

All this means that you now have another corporate function to mesh into the sales cycle: hosting. And hosting for a corporate customer does not simply mean a PC under a desk somewhere running your software connected to the Internet. Corporate customers will demand a robust service, as Adrian King, COO of Nimbus explains:

> *"The effort of hosting your own software for customers is not something you should underestimate. Whilst you don't need to own the datacenter and hardware, you do need to control every-thing else. Corporate customers will expect security, back-up and resilience at least as good as their own internal IT departments. And depending on the sensitivity of their data that you are storing for them, the security may be even more stringent. Plus they will expect to audit you.*
>
> *But the benefits of hosting in a Value Created world are stark. Our revenue growth has grown 40% per year since offering host-ing, compared with 5% before. Sales cycles have dropped by 3–6 months. And we have less burn-out of professional services staff as they can support customers without having always to travel to customer sites."*

Finance

Running a Value Created company is massively cash-constrained. Sales cycles are long, the high-margin product purchases are at the back end of the engagement, so cash collection is critical. This is a role that Finance should play. Whilst it is tempting to put the onus 100 percent on the salesmen, they are trying to position themselves as trusted advisor and this does not fit well with the image of credit collection. Therefore they need to ensure that there is Purchase Order cover for any work before it is started. The work gets done, the mentor promised to sort out the Purchase Order, but it's not a priority. Eventually it becomes too difficult or embarrassing to keep chasing the mentor and risks damaging the relationship. So there is pressure by the salesman to write it off. And so you slip into high levels of unpaid professional services. You do need to keep the salesmen accountable, and one approach is to pay salesmen their commission 100 percent on payment or if you are more lenient, 50 percent on Purchase Order and 50 percent on payment. This seems to focus them better.

The key metrics for Finance for the Value Created part of the business are debtor days, cash in bank, and backlog. Backlog is professional services days, hosting, or software support which has Purchase Order cover but has not been delivered. However, just because it hasn't been delivered doesn't mean that you cannot invoice it and be paid. It is just that it cannot be accrued in the accounts.

If you are running a major corporation you will have multiple operational cultures, but probably only one Finance team. So it's critical that they understand the dynamics of the Value Created sale so that they can support the business. To the uneducated Finance manager Value Created looks like a badly managed, out-of-control Value Added operation run by mavericks.[50]

SAFETY NOTES

First of all we need to give you one or two[51] words of warning, both about working with customers and driving change.

The incompetent customer

We have made one assumption throughout this book so far, which is that all customers follow the IMPACT process in a competent way. They all

---

[50] They may be right, but that is no reason to allow them to close you down!!
[51] Well technically – four points and 2000+ words.

follow the IMPACT process. We all do. None of us can avoid doing so as it's human nature, but do we all do it in a thorough way?

 Most suppliers and customers have not heard of buying cultures, operational cultures, and the IMPACT process.

Remember how we described the major difference between early adopters and early majority as being the degree of risk which they are willing to accept. Early adopters don't miss out steps in the IMPACT cycle, they just move far more rapidly. What do we get if customers move through the phases without recognizing the degrees of risk involved for a particular initiative? We get an incompetent customer, and these are very dangerous animals!

This incompetence can reveal itself in many ways from simple over-eagerness, all the way to cultural dysfunction across a siloed organization. But how it reveals itself is not the issue. The big issue is that the incompetent customer can cost you time, money, reputation, and heartbreak. There are so many examples of the incompetent customer – from people and organizations we have worked with that have given us scars. Here is one which expresses the symptoms and results very well:

We were working with a customer, a hi-tech manufacturer with an increasingly complex partner ecosystem, who had done some Identification work and had realized that they needed to drive closer relationships with key partners in their main industry sectors. A mentor was found in the Channel Operations group, which is a logical place for the mentor to be found. The mentor started the Identify phase by creating a small virtual team involving an experienced Channel Manager, a Project Manager, Channel Marketing, and me as an external consultant. We all agreed that this was not an issue of training the Channel sales teams but something that had a structural foundation (operational culture alignment). Our recommendation was that the first thing to be done was to create a common process framework to drive a different way of working for the Channel Partners. All supports tools, collateral, and system would be accessed in the context of the end-to-end processes – branded the Intelligent Operations Manual (IOM). So far, so good. The project then moved into the Position stage and this is where the wheels started to come off. The mentor had underestimated the funding required to deliver this project and a struggle for control of the project began. In fact, it was not so much a struggle as a game of poker with the different interested parties continually upping their ante in the bid for ownership. Over the space of two months the interested parties inside the customer blossomed so we could never get them together at one time. Now the project extended to several different supplier offerings, each of whom was convinced they could do everything on their own, but not in the context of the IOM which got lost in the fight for control. The assembled rabble was dragged into the Assessment stage in the form of a pilot program which had structure without the IOM. It will not surprise you to learn that at this point the whole project crashed and burned at a significant cost to the customer in both financial and reputational terms.

Sadly this is not a rare example as we hear of similar cases on a weekly basis. The root cause is that the mentor in the customer does not understand the IMPACT process and the risk assessment required before moving from one phase to the next. But there is a simple answer – give them a copy of this book.

A second example illustrates dysfunctional silos and comes from a customer[52] which had done some Identify with a well-known global strategic consultancy:[53]

> *The customer had seen that there was significant opportunity for them to approach a growing market with a vertical strategy. The first thing they did was to create vertical sales teams, then wait to see what would happen. Not much. So a mentor was found in the form of a senior Sales Director who engaged me because he was aware of the risks of verticalization. Again, so far so good. The mentor then went looking for budget for the implementation and found it in the Learning and Development (L&D) department, whose particular buying culture was Value Offered. So my first contact from them was a request for a 'product overview' with costs. My reply of "What product?" produced blank stares and a repeat of the question. Anyway, so there we were. At the Mentor phase with a mentor thinking that their job was done even though they had not engaged a sponsor. The budget-holders sitting at Transaction phase feeling that I was uncooperative.*
>
> *Our original estimate was that we should have had an implementation project through a pilot and into the field within two months. After two months playing telephone ping-pong with the L&D folk we decided that the best thing to do would be to work with them since they were budget-holders. We completed statements of work, purchase orders were issued, and a 'product' was designed. What then followed was a long, tortuous, and repetitive cycle of presenting the product to one stakeholder at a time who wanted changes made. It was all very messy and there was still no firm date for implementation.*

---

[52] You may be thinking "Why doesn't this guy name the company?" But if you were the company would you want to be named here?

[53] So, so tempting but I can't mention their name either.

At the point we were about to give up a new mentor arrived on the scene who took the project back to the Mentor stage. He did a thorough stakeholder analysis with us, during which we identified and engaged with a strong sponsor. The result was that we completed the Assessment pilot and built the Case and agreed the project at Transaction within four weeks. Result!

Sales Compliance vs. Sales Engagement – confused?

Many companies, in an attempt to get their operational culture better aligned to the customers' buying cultures, make the common error of confusing Sales Compliance with Sales Engagement and placing all their focus and effort upon Sales Compliance:

- **Sales Compliance** is the structural element of the sales organization. It will be made up of planning methodologies and templates, supported by a technology platform which could be anything from a home-made Sales Force Automation tool in Excel to an all-singing, all-dancing application like Seibel.
- **Sales Engagement** is the process-driven behavioral engagement with the actual customers. This is interaction of the customers and supplier from a buying perspective. This is IMPACT.

Suppliers think about the sales engagement and decide that it can be fixed by implementing more and more sales compliance. Instead, they should be looking at the overall sales engagement, the operational processes, and then providing the tools and systems to support and reinforce the engagement.

What the implementation of a sales compliance model can do for many companies is create a sense of busyness; everyone is reporting everything, metrics are applied, forecasting is more thorough, resources are quantified, and nobody has free time in their diaries. Sadly, busyness is not productivity and customers become aware of this when the supplier's sales engagements are driven by the supplier's own triggers and reporting cycles, "... tell me Mr Customer, do you have a compelling event?" Some customers become savvy to these triggers, especially at period ends, and learn how to control the supplier – much like Pavlov's dog.[54]

The integration of a sales compliance model with a sales engagement process can be demonstrated very simply. The integrated model looks like Fig 9 below:

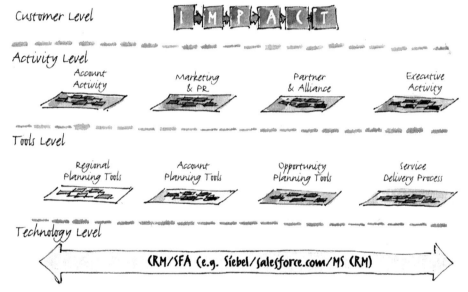

Fig 9: Sales engagement and sales compliance.

This shows the structural perspective of an integrated and aligned operational culture. By having IMPACT as the highest level process it no longer matters that all the silos of activity have different rituals and

[54] One enterprise sales guy makes 100% of sales in the last month of his financial year. He always hits his target, despite giving 85% discounts. But it's the same every year. He knows it. His customers know it.

habits, nor that they use different tools to manage their data. Because when it comes to issues concerning selling to a customer, there is a single unifying process for communication and measurement – IMPACT. This structural model is the same for all companies regardless of size, all that changes is the complexity. If you are a start-up, your technology level will probably consist of Outlook. Your tools level may be your memories of training courses you have been on in the past.[55] Your activity level will be the combined day–to-day efforts of you and your founding partner, but the customer level never changes because the IMPACT process never does. The four buying cultures are out there waiting for you.

Implementing a vertical strategy

This year's announcement at the sales conference was that the company was going to become more customer-intimate and that the company would focus on five vertical sectors (typically Financial Services, Manufacturing, Telecommunications, Public Sector, and Commercial). After the strategy is announced comes the new structure, in which sales people are given new account portfolios which will consist of accounts from just one sector. Sales support will have a vertical flavor too. Marketing will take up the torch and include phrases such as ". . . for your banking needs . . ." or ". . . one of our manufacturing customers improved productivity by 500% . . ."

One year later the vertical strategy does not seem to have made much difference, except to increase the cost of selling, so the company sets about recruiting specialists from the chosen sectors in the belief that deep knowledge of the sector will improve sales in the chosen verticals, even though this pushes up the cost of selling further. Meanwhile the existing (or remaining) sales people will be trained in how to talk to the executive level in the sector in the belief that being able to reference balance sheet terminology will grab the attention of business executives.

---

[55] What did the O in SCOTSMAN stand for?

Two years later still the sales organization appears to be very different on the outside, but what about the perception of the customers and the brand of the company? The sad truth is that the customers will perceive little difference from the way they were sold to before, and the brand equity of the supplier will be much the same as it ever was.

What a waste of time! Why do companies do it? At the end of a great deal of expense and hard work all that has changed are the salesman's territories. From our experience there are many reasons companies give for going vertical, apart from desperation and me-too behavior. The most common include, in no particular order of importance:

- A need to be different.
- To get closer to the customers.
- To get more depth in what appears to be a rich sector.
- To create larger revenue streams from individual customers.
- To create value through intangible assets such as brand and networks.

The fundamental flaw in all these arguments is that vertical, horizontal, matrixed, or doughnut makes not a jot of difference if your operational culture is not aligned with the customer's buying culture.[56] If you are thinking of implementing a vertical sales strategy, stop, go straight to Chapter 7 of this book, don't collect $200, and apply the OCA Methodology before it's too late. You have been warned!

The partner ecosystem was an after-thought

Since your partner ecosystem should be an integral part of your operational culture, it is no surprise to know that the alignment of your partners involves all the same issues as getting the direct sales teams pointed in the same direction. The only thing is that it's even worse because you do not have direct control.

---

[56] But you probably know that if you've read this far through the book.

We saw a situation with a large network equipment manufacturer just after the dotcom bubble burst, who realized that future stability would come from more Value Created engagements with customers. The nature of their product offering meant the partner ecosystem was going to be critical to these new engagements. When they analyzed the 4000 or so partners which they had in Europe, they concluded that there were only 46 with Value Created capabilities. The implications of this were far more than just an inability to deliver their own strategy. They had to change or dump 3954 partners. Making the change to align the partner ecosystem and get resources working in the right place was a leadership task which took some courage![57]

If you understand which portion of the business is reliant upon partners for success, then you can segment this into the buying cultures. By using a similar process we can analyze our partner ecosystem by buying culture too. Very often the output looks something like the Fig 10 below. The left-hand column is the business by volume split across the buying cultures. The right-hand column is the partner activity. This is not an atypical situation. The reason for this is that partner ecosystems are rarely designed or constructed in a thought-out way. They just form organically, rather like bacteria growing on a drainpipe.

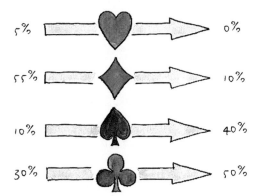

Fig 10: Buying culture volume split

[57] And a lot of unplanned budget.

How scary is the misalignment? Value Captured is 5 percent of business but we wouldn't expect partners support. However 55 percent of our business is Value Created with only 10 percent of our partners activity. This means we will fail to scale. Value Added and Value Offered we have partners tightly after too few leads. And if we are trying to transition to a more innovative model we will struggle as 90 percent of partners activity is locked in the past Value Added and Offered.

Value Added partners who have invested in the relationship may start to feel tied to the partnership and feel very let down by the supplier's current strategy. They don't believe the partner is working with them, trust is low, and they will feel there is little opportunity (and little reason) for further commitment. Value Created partners, such as they are, will feel that they are chronically under-funded and resourced by the supplier, and yet they probably realize how critical they are to the supplier's business strategy.

Armed with this knowledge you can design and build a partner ecosystem.

CHAPTER 6

So what can I do about it?

CEO

As CEO you are responsible for the overall performance of the business, so the buck stops with you. You need a framework for you and your executive team to make the critical decisions about which business model or models to employ.

Getting a real understanding of the concepts and implications of the different buying cultures is the starting point. Only you can sponsor the top-down analysis of the propositions vs. sales cultures to get some hard data to establish whether you need to take action.

Now, your actions will vary. If you are the CEO of a major multinational you are probably reading this from the comfort of your private jet. If so, then the simplest approach is probably to get your PA or Business Manager to order a copy of this book for each member of the top two tiers of management and your Board. Get them to read it and be ready to present back the implications at the next quarterly executive or Board meeting.

The topics for discussion should be:

- Analysis of propositions vs. buying cultures.
- Alignment of sales teams vs. buying cultures.
- Organization and support from the rest of the organization.
- Implications on planned and future M&A.
- The future strategy of innovation or incubation programs.

If you are slightly more down to earth, then the same approach applies but you probably need to order fewer books – and you have to do it yourself.

If you are the CEO of a start-up then your situation is very different and is discussed next.

CEO OF A START-UP

You need to maximize the sales of your innovative, paradigm-shifting, trend-shifting product before the competition catch up and the big players steal the idea. Therefore, you should be assuming that you have a Value Created sale and be looking to disprove it. You have probably already hired a hotshot big-ticket salesman who is Value Added through and through. Therefore, you have a 'non-believer' in your midst. So any research about the market, your approach, and sales cycles needs to keep him out of the loop until you have firm evidence.

Once you've established that you really are Value Created, it is time to go about educating the rest of the team on the approach. The best approach is probably a face-to-face presentation, or a workshop. Simply reading this book is not immediate and 'in yer face' enough to change your sales-men's deeply rooted instincts.[58]

---

[58] Sometimes the only approach is a mutually agreed split.

The danger is that if you don't get this sorted out now when you are fairly small, you may not get to be big – unless you are very well funded. Alternatively, you do grow and start recruiting salesmen who are Value Added and you are simple prolonging the agony and eventual death. The only savior is the market. If your market matures really quickly you may suddenly find yourself in a Value Added market. Then you probably have the right sales team and business model. But if you are not the gorilla in the market you may have a torrid time competing against the market leader. Then the only place of safety is in a niche that you can protect well. Not a good starting point for global domination and that massive IPO or trade sale so that you can buy that company jet you've been promising yourself.

Interestingly, you may have stumbled into a Value Created sales technique unknowingly. Guy Kawasaki puts it beautifully in his latest book, *The Art of the Start*.

There are two approaches:

- One approach is the product guys (founders) develop the product and the sales guys (founders) hit the street. After 3 months of limited sales but lots of requests for help in terms of consulting, the consultants (same founders) do consulting work which eventually generates a need for the product and the company uses the consulting revenue to grow the company.
- The second approach is similar. The founders do consulting work which eventually generates a need for the product and the company uses the consulting revenue to grow the company. This approach simply reduces the time to get to the same answer.

CHIEF OPERATIONS OFFICER

As you are responsible for optimizing the operation of the entire business, this is pretty fundamental. The only difficulty is that often sales is outside your remit. You know that sales are made by more than just the sales teams, but you need to engage the Sales Director. However, before you do that, you can get together the analysis to understand the size of the problem. Is it 80 percent of the business that should be Value Created, or only 15 percent? How aligned is your partner channel?

What you may discover is why your teams are working so hard, but not getting the results that they deserve. R&D are churning out changes which the sales guy says he needs to close a deal. Marketing is struggling to keep up with the different requests for marketing collateral, lead generation, and market data. And the professional services guys are run ragged. All these are symptoms of a lack of alignment between your customer's buying cultures and your operational culture.

Once you have your supporting evidence you need to explore the principles of buying cultures, IMPACT, and operational cultures with the Sales Director.[59] Together, once you've conducted the analysis, the questions you should be asking are:

- What is the spread of propositions across buying cultures?
- How does this impact the alignment of sales teams to buying cultures?
- What are the correct organization and incentive programs?
- How will we address 'internal channel conflict' between Value Created salesmen and Value Added salesmen in the same customer?
- How will we get support from the rest of the organization: pre-sales, support, professional services?

SALES DIRECTOR

Again it depends on the size of your organization, the span of products, and your background. If you are Sales Director of a major multinational you will have a wide range of products with an equally broad spread of history and market maturity. Most will be split between Value Offered

---

[59] Light blue touch paper and retire.

and Value Added. The analysis of proposition vs. buying culture will need to be conducted by country, as every product or proposition will be at a different state of maturity in each region.

So, the starting point is a critical analysis, sponsored by you with support from your CEO and ideally your peers, as it has an impact across the entire operation. Once you've conducted the analysis, the questions you should be asking are:

- What is the spread of propositions across buying cultures?
- How does this impact the alignment of sales teams to buying cultures?
- What are the correct organization and incentive programs?
- How will we address 'internal channel conflict' between Value Created salesmen and Value Added salesmen in the same customer?
- How to get support from the rest of the organization: pre-sales, support, professional services?

HEAD OF M&A

Your job is to buy companies for the organization and then sell off the bits that don't fit with the overall corporate strategy. Some research on the current portfolio of products may throw up some very interesting data. How much does the spread of products across buying cultures support the statements about innovation in last year's annual report?

The analysis can help you formulate your M&A strategy and dovetail it with the overall corporate strategy. The questions that should be debated at executive team level are:

- What is the target percentage distribution of products in each of the different buying cultures?
- What is the percentage split now and over what time period do we want to get to our target distribution?

- How do I value different products – now and their lifetime value?
- What products can I acquire which appear to be underperforming in other companies because they are being sold against the wrong buying culture?
- Before I buy that new innovative start-up with a really sexy new product, is the company geared up to sell an innovative product?

HEAD OF MARKETING

As with sales, the size and complexity of your company will have implications for what operational culture alignment means to you as Head of Marketing, but there are some principles which don't really ever change. The Value Offered and Value Added space is a defined market. A zero-sum gain. If you grow your market share it's at the expense of your competitors.

The huge opportunity is the Value Created sale. Why so big? This is the space where new markets are created. So what is the role of marketing here? This space is generally created and won by specialist teams driving powerful thought-leadership. The smart money has strategic marketing at the sharp end of these teams because this growth is usually opportunity-led.

INVESTORS OR VCS

Before you invest in a company, does it have the correct business model and operational culture? A pretty fundamental question. But simply asking the management of the company you are about to invest in is probably not enough. They are hardly going to say that they didn't have the correct business model. So how are you going to validate that they have?

Clearly this is not the only due diligence. You still need to evaluate the management team, the product, the market, and the competition. But now you have another lens or perspective which will make you ask some different questions throughout the due diligence:

- How attuned is the management team to the different buying cultures?
- Is the product, or the target markets for the product, likely to be Value Added or Value Created?
- Are the management and sales team hard-core Value Added or consultative Value Created?
- Is the competition aligned with their buying cultures, or is there an opportunity to sneak an advantage?
- If there is misalignment between the company's operational culture and the market buying culture, can you influence it to dramatically scale the company?

A fairly simple, quick, and relatively unobtrusive approach would be to do the analysis of product/proposition vs. buying culture. This will give you a clear view on their alignment and massively de-risk your investment.

An alternative approach is to apply the same analysis to your existing portfolio. How many of the companies with great products failed to meet expectations when you invested? Have you and your management simply written them off as part of 'portfolio investing'. Portfolio investing is the view that you get some stars and some dogs. Sometimes you cannot legislate which are going to be stars or dogs. So a good investor makes so much on the stars that the dogs don't matter to the portfolio.

What if that were not 100 percent true? You don't invest in dogs. You perform weeks of expensive due diligence to avoid the dogs. You hope to pick only stars – so what goes wrong? What if you could help the dogs become stars, just by applying the buying culture and IMPACT principles?[60]

---

[60] You start by giving them each a copy of this book. If they don't bother to read it, you have some clues about their desire to do whatever it takes to succeed.

HEAD OF INNOVATION

Your title gives the game away. You are there to be innovative. And if the company can afford to have a Head of Innovation, it's probably a relatively large and mature business. You will have a portfolio of products and your role is to bring in new innovative products. So, a couple of questions:

- What does innovative mean?
- How is success going to be measured?
- Where are the innovative products going to come from?

So if your role is to look for innovative products in the market and acquire them, then you should look back at the Head of M&A and Investors & VCs sections.

If your role is to generate innovative ideas internally across the whole company then the question is, "How will the new, sexy, innovative products be taken to market?" The answer to that question is arguably more important than "Where do the ideas come from?" But this is where innovations teams seem to spend their time – trying to get the workforce to generate new ideas.

How are you going to take the products to market? Will it be through the existing sales teams? If so, then you should by now have realized that you have a problem. If you are able to establish separate businesses spun off to market, sell and support the new product then great. If not, how do you ensure that the operational culture of the business is aligned with the buying cultures? Particularly when the vast majority of the revenue (and hence the perceived value) of the company is probably Value Added. And your exec team doesn't want their Value Added revenue stream at risk and the resulting drop in share price to be a result of your new (insignificant), yet innovative product.

However, this is the biggest risk in taking new innovative products to market from within a large corporation. But innovation is critical to sustainable success. Apple innovates aggressively so that it obsoletes its own products rather than waiting for a new entrant to steal a march.

But it is very difficult to launch a new product when the existing business is going well. This is what Charles Handy calls the Sigmoid Curve or Second Curve thinking in his excellent book, *The Empty Raincoat*.[61] In summary, Handy suggests that any product (like life, an empire, or a business) starts slowly and builds up, peaks, and declines. But way before it peaks, at Point A in the Fig 11 below, you need to be developing the next product because it will take time to get up to speed. But how do you know where Point A is? It should be before the original product peaks, but how can we know when that is? The perfect time is probably when all the messages are that the original product is going well and still accelerating. Only once the product starts to decline do we know that we should have started the new product some months earlier. But by then it's too late. See the problem?

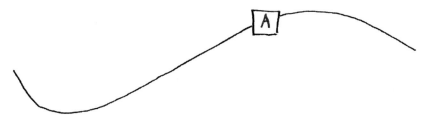

Fig 11: Charles Handy's Sigmoid curve

It's a paradox in some ways, when we say the time to change is when things are going well. But as Bill Shankly – the late, great, and very successful Liverpool football club manager – once famously said: "Always change a winning team."

---

[61] A summary of the book is in the Appendix.

CHAPTER 7

Always change a winning team

CAN YOU HAVE TOO MUCH SUCCESS?

Maybe you're growing at 50 percent. You're the market leader. But that never stopped Toyota constantly striving to innovate. Could you grow at 150 percent? What we are aiming for is not the British understated "Well, we did quite well." It's the American "We annihilated them – left them in the dust."[62]

Remember back to *Crossing the Chasm*. When the market matures and companies cross the chasm there can only be ONE gorilla. Everyone else is a monkey. Only the largest, strongest, and most successful (by whatever measure the market determines) will be the gorilla. And it's only the gorilla who will have outrageous growth and profit margins. Examples of this are Microsoft (operating systems, Office), Google (online ads), SAP (enterprise software), Oracle (databases), Apple (music players). The reason you've worked your nuts off with an innovative product with razor thin margins is to become the gorilla. So you need to make sure that you are performing at the top of your game, so you guarantee that you are the gorilla when the market changes.

---

[62]Punch the air defiantly. High fives all round. You get the idea.

Andy Berry, General Manager at Fuji Xerox Global Services, shows that the largest and most successful companies worry about this stuff every day:

> *"We had all the elements of a market leader – a strong, industry-leading solution, highly skilled staff and proven success with many blue chip corporate and Government clients. However, we suffered from many of the challenges of a fast growing business – our clients were continually pushing us to create new value for them. Our internal teams had grown quickly and were becoming increasingly siloed. Legacy business processes were slowing down our ability to translate innovation into practical outcomes. To hit our growth targets we needed to address these issues and align everyone within the business closer to our clients and the industries they operate in."*

SO, ARE YOU PERFORMING?

Part of the problem of innovative products is that they are probably unique, so there is nothing to compare against – nobody to use to benchmark performance. So a little quiet soul searching, aided and abetted by the vital signs in Chapter 4, may help you decide if you are underperforming. Sometimes whole industries fail to react when, with hindsight, it was glaringly obvious that some sort of change was needed. Take the case of the mobile telephone operators. Chris Huggett, Sales VP at 3Com, reflects on the challenges of an entire industry – the mobile telco industry:

> *"Mobile telephone operators do two things really well. They find customers and negotiate airtime contracts. They have an operation which is geared to getting the customers on board, porting their numbers to their network, doing the legal contracts and dealing with the billings. The mobile operators do all that extremely well. The challenge is that the price of their product goes down 15%*

every year to the point where one day it will be free. Right now it's close to free. Some of the deals mobile operators have done with large business customers like investment banks are effectively free for domestic calls, and they charge more for roaming (though the EU has attacked that too). They are in a world where their core product is going to become effectively free with voice over IP and Skype on mobiles. The mobile operators' core business was and is under attack.

So how does that translate in terms of what mobile operators should be doing? Well, potentially what they should be doing is engaging with customers on 'mobility' rather than on 'mobiles'. This means instead of saying "we can sell you airtime" they could be offering their opinion about the things in the customers' organizations which need to be mobilized: ERP systems, email systems, all sorts of business applications. Also, they should offer their opinion about how to get maximum productivity out of a highly mobile workforce by putting versions of those applications on some sort of mobile device. Now the mobile operators would have a real conversation of possibilities. Customers need basic connectivity but more importantly than that they will need someone to manage the desktop and the palmtop environment which will now include 4 or 5 critical applications. If the mobile operators' customers buy into this they are significantly less likely to switch to another network. How could they? The IT director will say "We can't switch to Vodafone when we've got all these things that need to be managed by T-Mobile. We'd have to change all of my key applications overnight, we can't do that, I won't let you.""

At a stroke this would solve the biggest problem in the mobile space, which is churn. So why haven't the mobile operators really gone out and done this when it seems such a no-brainer? It's because the machinery of state inside many mobile operators has suddenly found every element of its existence under threat. People who write the contracts for those customers say, "I don't know how to write the contract for that kind of business." The sales people say, "I don't know even who I would talk to. What I would say?" In short, the entire operation would need to be re-engineered. But at this rate Skype (and others) will solve the problem by putting them out of business.

So, every great achievement starts with a small committed decision.[63] Chapter 6 started to give you some ideas of what actions you could take, based on your role and your company. Now you need to decide to do something. Actions speak louder than words.[64]

---

[63] So profound it should be on a Successories (www.successories.com) poster along with a sycophantic picture - or maybe on the polar opposite and very funny Despair Inc. (www.despair.com).
[64] Which is a humbling admission coming from a couple of authors.

TRANSFORMATION – THE OCA METHODOLOGY

From the experience of 15 years' research and countless client engagements, we have identified a five-step methodology – which is called the Organizational Culture Alignment (OCA). But you should give it an emotive name which means something for your business, such as Project Diamond. These steps build on everything that we have discussed in the earlier chapters, but set them out in a practical blueprint for ACTION.

This methodology is all about transformation. Transforming you from your current mess of operational cultures to an organization where the products are correctly aligned. This is not the sales methodology that your sales teams follow. It is the steps to get you from where you are to where you need to be.

The methodology will help you understand where you are in terms of operational culture vs. the correct buying culture, and then realign your operation, building the operational culture and then getting it adopted and engrained into your organization. Sounds simple? It's a major analytical and transformational activity – but the prize is worth the effort.

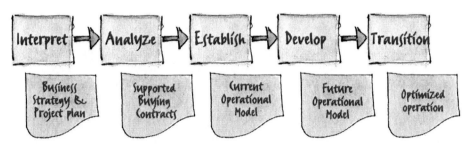

Fig 12: OCA Methodology

The OCA methodology has five steps:

- Interpret business strategy.
- Analyze sales mix.

- Establish current structure and resources.
- Develop best practice.
- Transition to the new world.

Of all the steps, the last is by far the most difficult, as any project manager of a major transformation program will tell you. It's a topic in its own right and (*blatant plug alert*) is covered in my first book, *Common Approach, Uncommon Results.*[65]

Let's think about each of the steps at a high level:

Step 1: Interpret business strategy

What are the key drivers to your business strategy? Markets, products, competition, appetite for risk and innovation. All these will determine how you need to change (if at all). You need to get support and buy-in from the executive team. Aligning to the buying cultures which drive the market is about an entire operational culture, not just changing the sales team or innovation team. Don't go on to Step 2 until you have at least a recognition within the executive team that a change is required, in the context of their business strategy.

Step 2: Analyze sales mix

You may have only one product selling into one market. Therefore, this is a relatively quick analysis of what buying culture should be used, and what buying culture is currently being used. If you have multiple products (X) being sold across different markets (Y), you have $X \times Y$ elements to analyze and match to one of the four buying cultures.

Step 3: Establish current structure and resources

You assess your current operation in terms of end–to-end processes and the organizational structure in terms of how you align your resources to

[65] A summary of the book can be found in the Appendix.

the four buying cultures. This assessment is across all the operational units, as they will all have some kind of responsibility within the sales engagement. You may not have all four buying cultures based on your product/markets.

Step 4: Develop best practice

For each buying culture that you need to use to sell your products, an operational culture needs to be developed in terms of people, process, and technology. These can be represented as a hierarchy of end-to-end processes with links to supporting information (tools, documents, systems). Every process step has a process owner. Metrics, where relevant,[66] can be attached to a process step. Comparing the models will help you establish which processes can be combined across the operational cultures. Alternatively, you keep them separate and essentially run the company as completely separate business units; one per operational culture.

Step 5: Transition to the new world

This is implementing your best practice model(s). Critically you need to take everyone in the organization with you, re-engineer elements of the business, and not kill the revenue stream and hence the business with it. This is open heart surgery in a speeding ambulance with a patient who isn't sure they want it done. So you need confidence that it can be done right first time.

Now let's explore each step in more detail, thinking about the key activities or what you need to do, how you can do it, and why you need to do it.

Step 1: Interpret business strategy

---

[66] I've see companies where they measure nothing and others where they measure everything. Both are wrong.

Key activities

This step assumes that your executive team has set out a clear business strategy. If not, then this step in the methodology is to develop your strategy:[67]

1. Define the timeframe of the business strategy you are working within.
2. Establish a clear definition of your product strategy (current and future) for the period of the business strategy. Don't forget that services are a product too.
3. Understand how you cut and dice your market. It does not matter how you do it, be it industry verticals, demographic types, technology usage or geographies, etc. Just so long as it's agreed.
4. Assess your brand equity from both a quantitative and a qualitative perspective. The image of an organization is inextricably linked to its operational culture models and hence its brand.
5. Understand how you defined your strategic customers or customer groups.
6. Agree which geographical areas you will cover for the purpose of this plan.
7. Extract the sales targets and goals from the business strategy.
8. Educate the leadership team in the principles behind the buying cultures, IMPACT, and the corresponding operational cultures.
9. Launch the project.

Deliverables

- A project plan, couched in terms of the business strategy.
- A mandate and sponsorship from the leadership team.

---

[67] And ask what the hell the exec team have been doing on their 3-day offsite strategy meetings – apart from improving their golf handicap?

Red flags

- Beware of those who have a vested interest in no change taking place. These may be people who are simply afraid of change, people for whom the change may mean hard work, or people who are incapable of comprehending the new world.
- Brand. Don't think that this is just for Coca Cola and Nike, because it applies to you far more than you know. Changing the emphasis of operational culture must not have a negative effect on the brand image. You need to understand what brand equity you have and how much goodwill you can leverage from this 'brand promise'.

Checkpoint/milestone

- Do you have a clear understanding of the business strategy?

Step 2: Analyze sales mix

Key activities

1. Create a grid with all your products on the X-axis (horizontal) and all your markets on the Y-axis (vertical). Each intersection point potentially represents a *sales initiative* which needs to be mapped to a buying culture.
2. Establish which buying culture (and hence operational culture) is related to each *sales initiative*.

3. Now create a second grid with the X-axis having columns for sales goals, strategic definitions, current revenue, total revenue potential, and buying culture. The Y-axis is each sales initiative from the first grid and the business strategy.
4. Use the sales goals and strategic definitions to weight the sales initiatives.
5. Group your sales initiatives by buying culture. You now know which buying cultures you need to support and which are the most important sales initiatives for each. You also have a perspective on the relative balance of current and potential revenue across the buying cultures.
6. Get agreement on which buying cultures are going to need to be supported. If some of these are not going to be supported then the options are to discontinue selling the sales initiatives in the unsupported buying cultures, or move them to a different (misaligned) buying culture.

Deliverables

- Supported buying cultures.
- Prioritized sales initiatives vs. buying culture.

Red flags

- This piece of work may need to be done twice. Firstly for your current sales mix and again for the future sales mix in your business strategy. Consider this As-Is and To-Be. If these are very different, then it's worth doing both pieces of analysis, but it will have an effect on the project timescales.

Checkpoint/milestone

- Do you have agreement for each buying culture that is going to be supported?

Step 3: Establish current structure and resources

Key activities

1. Define and agree what the key processes are in your own value chain.[68] Think of your core end-to-end process, e.g. Quote to Cash, and then the supporting processes. That will drive out the key process steps and the organizational groupings associated with each step.
2. Create a grid with IMPACT laid out as 6 rows on the X-axis and your organizational groupings down the Y-axis.
3. At each step of IMPACT define what responsibilities each organizational grouping has today for each supported buying culture. When we say responsibility we mean formal responsibility which is something they are measured on, rewarded for, or fired for failing on.

Deliverables

* High level end-to-end process of the current operation.
* IMPACT responsibility matrix.

Red flags

* The easiest and quickest way to drive out the current operation is in live workshops. See the Appendix for ideas on running workshops. Don't be persuaded to create them as a series of interviews.

---

[68] If in doubt here, please refer to Michael Porter's work on the Value Chain. Just kidding. A simple end-to-end process will do.

The power of the workshop is that everyone's fingerprints are on the work, so there is shared ownership. It may be easier with an external facilitator.

- Be very aware of people who, at the start, thought that this was going to be a comfortable process mapping/flipchart session with a nice buffet lunch. Right now they will be starting to realize the implications of what is going on. The more senior the audience, the more difficult it is for them to think in terms of processes.

Checkpoint/milestone

- Do you have an agreed (and shared) view of the current business operation and responsibilities?

Step 4: Develop best practice

Interpret → Analyze → Establish → **Develop** → Transition

Key activities

1. Each supported buying culture requires different alignment of support and resources – i.e. operational culture. The operational culture needs to be described in terms of "what people have to do, how they do it, the tools they need to do it, and how they are measured". This is captured as a hierarchical end–to-end process model; one for each buying culture/operational culture that you agreed to support. The top-level process diagram will probably be very similar for each operational culture, so you need to go down two or three levels to drive out the differences.

2. Every process step on the models should have a resource/organizational unit (process owner) associated with it, and where needed a metric/KPI. Adding these will validate the processes.

3. Unless you are going to operate as completely parallel business units, one for each operational culture, you now need to look for processes that can be shared. Be careful that you combine them based on the activity, not the resource. The metrics will give you some clues. Same-sounding activities with very different metrics may mean they cannot be combined.

4. Build the combined hierarchical end-to-end process model for the company. This includes the elements of the processes for each operational culture that cannot be shared, and the shared services. This is the new target operating model or *intelligent operations manual* for the business. Unless you only have one buying culture to align to, it will look more complex than the current business. That is because it now reflects the different ways that you need to work to align your teams to the buying cultures.

5. For each process step in the intelligent operations manual attach process-related content: documents, policies, templates, links to systems, training material. This is the 'sales compliance' (process-related content) overlaid on top of the 'sales engagement' (operations manual).[69]

Deliverables

- A combined hierarchical end–to-end process model (intelligent operations manual) for the company.

Red flags

- Again, the easiest and quickest way to drive out the different process maps is in live workshops. These are too important to be created

---

[69] If none of this makes sense, then you must have missed the section at the end of chapter 5 on "Sales Compliance vs. Sales Engagement".

based on a series of interviews. The power of the workshop is that you are starting the change management effort. The workshop attendees are starting to form an agreed model for the new ways of working. Again, it may be easier with an external facilitator as it can get quite emotional.[70]

- Be very precise as to which organizational group is responsible for each process step. Initially people will not want to volunteer themselves.
- Driving out KPIs for process steps can get very emotive. We are talking about the A word – accountability.
- Reassure people involved that the models being designed will not be implemented tomorrow (not unless your business plan dictates 100 percent strategic change this week).

Checkpoint/milestone

- Do you have a mandate to change the operation of the company? To implement the new, intelligent operations manual?

Step 5: Transition to the new world

Key activities

1. In Step 3 you developed the current operations model. In Step 4 you created the future operations model. The first activity is to understand

---

[70]The facilitator is to keep the momentum going, ensure everyone is engaged and contributing. Not just hand out the tissues.

the gap, cost the implications, and develop a plan to transition to the new operations model. The plan will cover organization changes, new systems or changes to systems, communication of transition, staff training in new operational processes, changing incentives and bonus structures, updating documents and collateral (including policies, procedures, marketing collateral, intranet, website), and updated budgets.

2. Agree the plan and timescales.

3. Deliver the plan.[71]

Red flags

- This plan must be built by the people who are going to have responsibility for implementing it. It cannot be a plan that is 'done' to people by senior management or external consultants, as that would guarantee failure.
- Beware of land grabs and empire builders!
- Beware the Teflon-coated ones!

USING THE OCA METHODOLOGY

As with every methodology, it should be used to structure the approach, not be applied rigidly. Every company has its own history, culture, and structure, and that means that some steps in the methodology need to be changed to make them work.

One company that took the methodology, tailored it, and applied it to drive a massive transformational change is Fuji Xerox Global Services (FXGS). FXGS is part of the $3.5bn revenue global document outsourcer, with over 6100 client sites across 50 countries. FXGS had set itself some significant strategic targets, not least of which was to continue to grow

---

[71] This is not a cop out. There is too much to cram into a paragraph or two. *Common Approach, Uncommon Results*, which is summarised in the appendix covers this in great detail.

revenue aggressively in specific industry verticals while containing costs of added staff, infrastructure, and overheads.

Andy Berry, General Manager At Fuji Xerox Global Services, takes up the story:

> *"We had all the elements of a market leader – a strong, industry-leading solution offering, highly skilled staff and proven success with many blue chip corporate and government client[s]. However, we suffered from many of the challenges of a fast growing business – our clients were continually pushing us to create new value for them. To hit our growth targets we needed to respond and align everyone within the business closer to our clients and the industries they operate in."*

The role of marketing in the change program was going to be key. Pam Fleming, FXGS Marketing Strategy Manager, continues the theme:

> *"We recognized that having a solid business plan was only a small part of the challenge. So often in large organizations, these plans get communicated and implemented ineffectively by the client-facing groups. The people that matter – our clients – see little or no meaningful change. We, with the support of consultants, developed a five stage program to guide us through the evolution of the operational culture change from start to finish."*

The five-stage program Pam refers to was delivered as a mix of consulting, planning workshops, and training. The first stage of operational culture alignment was for the leadership team to define the market strategy for each targeted industry. With representatives from every business and support function including F&A, Legal, and HR, they mapped the products (Lines of Service) onto the vertical industries and established the correct sales engagement model – Value Offered, Value Added, Value

Created, or Value Captured. They then established how each FXGS business unit should realign their operational culture to the correct sales engagement model.

Having defined the structural alignment plan for the products, markets, and organization, at the second stage the sales and marketing leadership team developed value strategies for selected products in each key industry vertical. This powerful approach allows industry insights to be captured, used, and communicated across client-facing teams in an efficient, scalable way. Pam Fleming continues:

> *"Marketing teams struggle to build and share industry knowledge effectively. Some businesses use research companies, others employ industry gurus. But all have difficulty keeping this industry information current and making it easy to use in a sales campaign, or measurable in a value-based contract. This process allowed us to quickly build structured, value-based messaging for our key verticals. The same process and messaging can then be used in sales campaigns all the way through to service delivery contracts."*

In the third stage the attitude of the leadership was addressed by educating all the departmental heads who were involved in sales and marketing in buying cultures and operational cultures. This was further reinforced by teaching them how to coach within the different operational cultures.

At stage four, Value Creation workshops enabled the sales, professional services, and post-sales teams to apply the industry insights that the marketing team had developed to key accounts. Because of the scalable nature of the Value Creation process, it was possible for customized versions of these workshops to be delivered to the service delivery teams, to give them the knowledge and skills to continually look for ways to cross-sell and create new value for clients.

In the fifth stage the leadership team focused on how to review progress and ensure successful execution of the implementation plan created at stage one. This was done in a workshop, where clear definition was placed upon the desired behaviors of client-facing personnel. The process-based metrics which would allow the leadership greater control over the pace and integrity of the changes being implemented. Pam Fleming added:

> *"The approach has allowed us to focus all our internal teams on delivering value. From marketing to operations, pre-sales to finance, each team is now able to clearly identify, quantify and communicate how they bring value to our clients."*

The results are staggering. Andy Berry sums up the benefits as:

> *"We achieved pretty well all we set out to achieve:*
>
> - *our average deal size trebled,*
> - *our largest deals are not only far bigger but there are more of them, and*
> - *our resource usage is much better aligned.*
>
> *On top of this the main benefit was speed.*
>
> *The insightful nature of the operational culture models was apparent from the start. Because of this the group was guided through the whole project very quickly and effectively.*
>
> *I've no doubt this is what delivered a quicker return to the business."*

The Final Word: A summary

You're a major corporation with a track record of strong sales for your current product or service. You've worked long and hard to produce a unique offering that you know the market needs. It should have flown out of the warehouse, but sales tanked and it has hit the morale and commissions of the sales team. Why?

Alternatively, you are a nimble start-up with experienced founders, who have built their reputation on sales in previous large corporations. Again, you've developed a ground-breaking innovation and made some early sales. To really ramp up revenues you have decided to sell through the channel, or you've hired a hotshot salesman. But nothing is happening. The only sales are being made by the founders. Why?

It has long been understood that different sales techniques are required depending on the type and maturity of the product, the industry, size of customer, and the market. Some people think 'sales is sales is sales', and that any good salesman can simply change or morph their technique to suit the particular circumstance. But over 15 years of research into business-to-business sales has shown that this thinking is fatally flawed. There are sales techniques, but these are fine-tuning. What really makes the difference are four clearly defined 'buying cultures'.

The maturity of the product in the customer's mind determines which of the four buying cultures is appropriate, and this is most stark in the purchase of technology or software. So, it is not surprising that there is a startling parallel between the buying cultures and the Technology Adoption Life Cycle principles that Geoffrey Moore made popular in his books *Crossing the Chasm* and *Inside the Tornado*, which focus on buying technology.

So, to transform your sales performance you first need to understand where your product is on the maturity curve. If your product is disruptive or innovative, it probably requires a Value Created sales approach to mirror the customer's buying culture. But what does this mean in terms of your company's operational culture, because the entire organization needs to be aligned to that culture?

The book paints a vivid picture of the operational culture of a company that is world class in selling innovation. It looks at it from every perspective: executive leadership, R&D, sales management and compensation, the 'sales animal', delivery and support. But the authors understand that most organizations firstly don't recognize that buying cultures exist and therefore have little or no alignment. So, set out in a very practical and implementable five-step methodology are the actions that any organization needs to take to assess their current position, analyze the market maturity, and then transform them to a proven business model. The end result is an organizational culture which is aligned with your customer's buying culture, and positioned for stellar sales growth. Got right, the results can be staggering.

So, the final word goes to Andy Berry, General Manager at Fuji Xerox Global Services, who sums up the benefits as: *"We achieved pretty well all we set out to achieve: our average deal size trebled, our largest deals are not only far bigger but there are more of them, and our resource usage is much better aligned. On top of this the main benefit was speed. I've no doubt this is what delivered a quicker return to the business."*

Enough said.

Appendix

This Appendix contains all the really best bits that didn't fit in the book. The Eden case study is fascinating as it isn't a typical 'supplier sells to customer' story. It's worth reading in full, but would have spoiled the flow of the book if we'd tried to insert it somewhere. The First Recovery case study is a great story highlighting Value Created sales in a competitive market.

Also, we've included other material which was referenced, but some of it is a little tangential to the main thrust of the book. We've also included summaries of the books we've referenced.

So in the Appendix we have:

- Case Study: Eden Project
- Case Study: First Recovery
- Book summaries
  - *Common Approach, Uncommon Results* by Ian Gotts and Richard Parker
  - *Crossing the Chasm* and *Inside the Tornado* by Geoffrey Moore
  - *The Empty Raincoat* by Charles Handy
  - *The Art of the Start* by Guy Kawasaki
- Article: Running senior-level workshops
- Article: Leading vs. lagging metrics

We are constantly updating the material on our website which you can download and may find interesting and useful as you start to apply the principles in the book: www.killer-products.com

May be you have a great success story from applying the principles. We'd love to hear about it. Or if you think of something that would have been really, really useful, then email us at feedback@killer-products.com.

CASE STUDY: EDEN PROJECT

This case study is the theory in practice. The Eden Project in Cornwall, England is known as a wonder of the modern world. It was the dream of Tim Smit who, from an idea in 1994, realized his dream in 2000. Eden is an international icon of sustainability and regeneration showing that mankind is capable of amazing things. The building is a model of cutting-edge architecture and technology, harvesting water and energy from the sun, wind, and rain to show how we all might live in the future.

Not only is the Eden Project an extraordinary phenomenon in itself, but the story of its creation is just as remarkable. If we follow its story, and look beyond the highly unusual nature of the fundraising, we will be able to see how this vast project followed the IMPACT process. It will also reveal some of the pitfalls which unaligned sales organizations can fall into.

The *Identify* stage started in the spring of 1994 when Tim Smit and two colleagues were inspired by a comment made by a visitor to Heligan Gardens in 1824. This comment had planted an idea in their heads – the idea of enormous glasshouses which could emulate the different temperate regions of the world. This idea was thought over and talked over for some months until in May 1994 they had a reasonably clear vision, or a 'big fat idea' as they called it, of five giant glasshouses linked together. Each glasshouse contained a unique environment which was a walk-through experience. At this point they had no idea how much the idea would cost, whether it could be built, or where there would be suitable land on which to build it. But what they did know was that the thinking needed to be refined in the *Identify* phase and one or more mentors found to drive everything forward. Tim Smit himself showed interest. He became the mentor, unconsciously self-appointed and by pure good fortune a suitable location, an old china clay pit called Bodelva, was offered up. It was ultimately to become the location which was to be used.

The "creation soup period" as Tim Smit called it was the *Mentor* phase and started in spring 1995. Tim had been responsible for the project which brought about the restoration of Heligan Gardens and now he used the network he had built up. These were the cooks of the creation soup. It was at this time that the virtual team of trusted advisors was created and some limited funding was acquired to enable the scoping of the project. The virtual team consisted of firms of architects, project managers, quantity surveyors, landscape architects, and environmental engineers. During the *Mentor* phase Tarmac, whose Chairman came from the region, donated funds and resources to the project with no strings attached, but Tarmac was a potential supplier. An act which shows the kind of financial risks involved when you engage customers early. But these are the risks that denote real partnership.

The initial business plan estimated that the project would cost £106 million; £50 million could come from the Millennium Commission, with another £20 million coming from other agencies. The rest needed to be found through private funding. The problem seen here was that to pay the interest on the loans for private funding the Eden Project would need one million visitors a year. This was a figure not just at the top of their estimations but way beyond their wildest imaginings.

The *Position* stage started in early 1996 when the Millennium Commission first visited the proposed site for Eden. In June 1996 a Project Manager was appointed. In the summer of 1996 the construction contract was placed in the *European Journal* for public tender. The bidders were Tarmac (not surprisingly), Hierry, Kier, McAlpine, Costain-Hochtief, and Bovis, all of whom started to make presentations. The final decision was not made until February 1997, and even then that was not a guarantee of business! In December 1996 the final proposed submission went to the Millennium Commission. The proposal contained detail on the whole scheme, costings, a business plan, an environmental impact assessment, documentation about the constructor, and a letter from the bank suggesting that if certain conditions were met they would be willing backers. On good advice the proposal had by now been remodeled as an application for £74.3 million (reduced from its original £106 million), and this reduction was to have significant and fortuitous results later on. On 23 May 1997 the Millennium Commission assigned the Trust a *conditional* award of £37.1 million and this meant that the Trust could move into a real stage of *Assessment* with confidence. This, as Tim Smit said, was the end of the old way of doing things as they now had to deliver a business plan which the Millennium Commission could believe in.

The *Assessment* stage opened with the banks negotiating with the Trust over the methods of funding and the equity stakes in Eden. The pressure was also on the Trust to complete the *Assessment* stage as both the constructor and the operator were impatient to sign their contracts. To expedite this, Eden implemented (in fact pioneered) what is now known as the New Engineering Contract (NEC). Using this they would be able to avoid the program and budget overruns usually associated with a project like Eden. It's a simple concept, whereby the Trust agreed the profit in advance with the constructor – thus allowing the contract to be run on an open book basis. It eliminates the ability of, and need for, the contractor to find fault with others as a way to create profit. To help make the NEC work well the Trust invited the constructor, McAlpine, to join their Board. The *Assessment* stage also flagged up the fact that Eden needed a proper Chief Executive who would be capable of working with the banks and the constructor. They also took on a full-time Finance Director at the same time.

The *Case* stage was busy as quite a few things had to be adapted to meet the needs of all the interested parties – from the Trust itself to the Millennium Commission and the banks providing the funding.

Many of these needs were still 'deal-breakers' even at this late stage. In September 1998 there was a meeting of all the stakeholders – the Government of the South West (representing the EU), NatWest Bank, McAlpine, and the Millennium Commission. At this meeting a serious deal-breaker to the business *Case* was resolved. This allowed the Millennium Commission to release funds for the purchase of the land on which Eden would be built. In October 1998 the Bodelva pit became the property of the Eden Project, but now came the huge challenge of addressing all the detail within the *Case*. The *Assessment* stage ended after the final round of due diligence was carried out in February 1999.

The *Transaction* phase started after the final due diligence and the contracts with NatWest Bank and McAlpine were signed. What then followed was one of the most remarkable construction projects to create an utterly remarkable building which tested new technologies. The biomes (glasshouses) are constructed from a tubular steel space-frame (hex-tri-hex) with mostly hexagonal external cladding panels made from the thermoplastic ETFE. At the outset, glass was proscribed due to its weight and potential dangers. The cladding panels themselves are created from several layers of thin UV-transparent ETFE film, which are sealed around their perimeter and inflated to create a large cushion. The resulting cushion acts like a thermal blanket to the structure. The ETFE material is resistant to most stains, which simply wash off in the rain. If required, cleaning can be performed by abseilers. Although the ETFE is susceptible to punctures, these can easily be fixed with ETFE tape. The structure is completely self-supporting, with no internal supports, and takes the form of a geodesic structure. The panels vary in size up to 9 m (29.5 ft) across, with the largest at the top of the structure. The ETFE technology was supplied and installed by Vector Foiltec, who is also responsible for ongoing maintenance of the cladding. The steel space-frame and cladding package (with Vector Foiltec as ETFE subcontractor) was designed, supplied, and installed by MERO (UK) plc, who also jointly developed the overall scheme geometry with the architect, Nicholas Grimshaw & Partners. The entire project was managed by McAlpine Joint Venture.

Grimshaws developed the geometry of the copper-clad roof in collaboration with a sculptor, Peter Randall-Page, and Mike Purvis of structural engineers SKM Anthony Hunts. It's derived from phyllotaxis, which is the mathematical basis for nearly all plant growth. The 'opposing spirals' are found in many plants such as the seeds in a sunflower's head, pine cones, and pineapples. The copper was obtained from traceable sources, and the Eden Project is working with Rio Tinto to explore the possibility of encouraging further traceable supply routes for metals, which would enable users to avoid metals mined unethically. The services and acoustic design were carried out by Buro Happold. There are a lot of innovative products and services in that list.

What started out as a dream for one man in 1994 became a reality, but only because the different parties (unwittingly) followed the IMPACT cycle.

You can read Tim Smit's full account of the Eden Project in his book, *Eden*

CASE STUDY: FIRST RECOVERY

Paul Jackson, Managing Director of First Recovery, explains how he used Value Offered, realized it wouldn't work, used Value Created, and now the market has matured is using Value Offered to grow his disaster recovery company. Not only has he crossed the chasm, but started to create its own tornado.

"I had the idea back in 1994 when I was at P&P. I was a Director with responsibilities all over the place and one of them was our rentals department. I was trying to think up new ways of using PC rentals. It was a profitable business but there was obviously scope to make it more profitable because you've got this kit sitting there not doing anything. So we had a brainstorm and disaster recovery was the answer. If a company has big problems and they need PCs in a hurry they are going to come to a rentals company, so why don't we pre-sell that as a contract.

Anyway the Board told me that was a load of old bollocks and they weren't interested so it didn't go any further. This was late '93 and I thought even then it was a great idea. But I got myself a proper job as Sales Director at Computer Associates. A few years later I was in one of life's hiatuses wondering what to do next and trying to work out what to do next and remembered the disaster recovery thing. I realized that what had changed between 1994 and 2002 was that the internet had come along and there were websites which show you where all the instant offices were, like Regus.

An entire industry had grown up which also hadn't existed in 1994. So, now I could set up easily. All I had to do was stick it together, find an investor and launch it, because I just knew a small business would buy it if I could price it keenly enough. There would be no competition because everyone else would send a consultant in, spend 3 days there, charge you $40,000. They would then sell you a seat in a centre somewhere $1,600 per seat per year minimum, which they'd also sell to 20 or 30 other companies and they'll charge you $1,600 per seat per year minimum. I thought that is a rip off, I can do better than that. What I could do now is for $800 a year for 6 seats.

As Rupert Murdoch once said, "Nobody ever lost money by going down market", so I packaged it and vanillarized it. I said this is what you are going to get, because every business in the immediate aftermath of a disaster needs the same things: somewhere to work from and all their technology: phones, internet, email. You put those together, packaged up dead cheap. Then add all the complicated bits to do with your specific software that runs your business. You've got to fix that as well but you need somewhere to do it, you need a platform. So that is what we give them, it's like being the paramedics. Pure Value Offered in a direct sales model.

When I had created a formal business plan there were two questions the main investor in First Recovery asked me: the first was, "Can you describe this tome in a simple short sentence, because if you can then you can sell it?" People don't have the attention span to have long complicated presentations given to them. I said it's "disaster recovery for small businesses". He said fine. Second question was, "Can you write out for me what you would see as a sales script in a typical sales situation?"

I wrote it in the style of Jeffrey Archer, you know ". . . he narrowed his piercing blue eyes, straightened his tie . . ." based around a conversation in a cold call situation. I created my imaginary customer, a Mr Shullbit who ran a PR agency in a little office in central London. The question was why on earth would the owner/manager of a little fashion PR company in London be interested in disaster recovery? So I developed in this conversation the reasons why it would be prudent for him to protect his business and that were he to fail to do so he would actually be failing his baby, because owner/managers see their businesses as I do with my own; "This is my bright, shiny jewel that I spend all my time polishing."

If somebody points out to you quite forcibly that it could all go "tits up" if you don't protect it, it's not going to cost you very much to do so, and you are failing in your duty to your baby. So, that was how that argument developed and overcame the investor's cynicism and I made the sale – at least in my book I had. I had an investor and we were ready to go. However, it had not escaped my notice that to make any money I was going to need to either talk to a quite extraordinary number of prospects or have an astonishing hit rate – or both!

What happened next was I had a conversation with a friend of mine who looked at my direct model and suggested going through insurance companies. But why would an insurer be interested in disaster recovery product? And of course very quickly it became apparent that they would be very interested because it alleviates their loss in the event of a disaster. In fact it's bloody obvious when you think about it. They pay out less than they otherwise would.

I originally thought this is a product which would be bought by those small business people. Find what their pains are and go, as I'd done with Mr Shullbit. But what I'd failed to understand was that the way to get owner/manager on side is to say that they not only can protect their baby, but hey! you can get it for free. Just choose this insurance company over that one and you get it as part of the package.

So, my friend introduced me to this chap who'd been an underwriter in the city for 25 years who agreed to come on board as a consultant to build a business model. The result was we signed our first and very signif-icant deal with AIG, November 2003, having opened our doors for trad-ing on 1 July 2003. The sales cycle with AIG was pure Value Creation: complicated, political and all about business value for AIG.

Now in 2008 we are about to accelerate because we are just about to launch a direct model; a direct version of First Recovery – Value Offered. We are going to send out about 10,000 mail-shots a month and the mail-shot will say to customers either you can buy this for $1,000 per year direct to First Recovery, or you can talk to our in-house insurance broker about buying an insurance policy which includes the DR offering for free. I think it's perfect.

The great thing is if we do get a lot of direct sales that produces a virtu-ous circle. It increases pressure on those insurers who haven't currently taken up First Recovery's service because they'll be losing business to those who have. That is what we really want to see."

BOOK SUMMARIES

Common Approach, Uncommon Results: How adoption delivers the results you deserve

By Ian Gotts and Richard Parker (2004), published by Ideas Warehouse

Common Approach, Uncommon Results reveals a proven approach which is simple and practical, and achieves staggering levels of adoption. It comes from the day-to-day experience of working with more than 500 organizations, including Lockheed Martin, Chevron, Toyota, Nestlé, JPMorgan, and Accenture BPO.

How do you really deliver results on all the initiatives and projects in your company? The answer is *Adoption*

Through *Adoption*, everyone in your company ensures that your strategy gets implemented and you obtain visible results from your initiative. Put succinctly:

$$R = IA^2 \ (\text{Results} = \text{Initiatives} \times \text{Adoption}^2)$$

Maximizing *Results* by successful *Adoption* of the transformational changes driven out of the *Initiatives*.

In other words, it does not matter how many initiatives (projects, exercises, programs, whatever) you throw at people if no-one adopts their results. Typical initiatives include Six Sigma, software implementation (SAP, Siebel, etc.), cost reduction, Sarbanes Oxley, and outsourcing programs.

While this may sound obvious, the corporate landscape is rife with these initiatives in progress, where little or no thought has been put into how to make sure that the rest of the organization actually adopt and own whatever improvement is advocated. Little surprise then that the adoption rate (and hence the success rate) of initiatives is pitifully low in many companies.

Gaining adoption is a challenge, not least because it involves changes in behavior and attitudes. Inspirational leadership helps kick-start adoption throughout the company, but it cannot sustain the necessary continuous improvement required for companies to stay competitive. Adoption has measurable results, as the dramatic benefits obtained by the success stories reveal.

Adoption means communicating the changes required of people – and getting people to make the changes. The approach we are suggesting is applicable to virtually every initiative and is achievable since it makes change as painless as possible. This is where a common language is required – an operational language which can describe the changes in activities, behavior, and results that are expected.

This language describes activities, roles, and measures, and is managed through the use of an Intelligent Operations Manual (IOM). It manages processes, documents, resources, and metrics – and the relationships between them. This is made possible by current IT infrastructure and software. Use of this IOM enhances accountability and serves to further adoption. And once the IOM is in place it can be applied to other initiatives and therefore increases their return on investment.

Whilst this may seem interesting in practice, most companies already have a range of initiatives at different stages. Therefore, the book takes five typical initiatives (outsourcing, Six Sigma, software package implementation, compliance, and rapid growth) and considers the most effective way of implementing the IOM alongside them depending on the phase of the initiative.

From the experience of countless client engagements we have identified seven simple steps to develop and manage the IOM. These steps build on the principles of adoption, but set them out in a practical blueprint for action. Once you have gone through these steps, it will be remarkable how the barriers to change seem to disappear. The current business issues of compliance, the introduction of enterprise software applications, and outsourcing all provide new challenges to business leaders. It is essential to get these right, and applying this new approach to these issues enables you to control and transform your business. It even keeps the strategy and your objectives to the fore when a business faces rapid growth.

Real case studies from clients around the world, in every industry, reveal the dramatic benefits and astonishing results achieved by putting this approach into action. For example:

- "We reduced the worldwide SAP implementation for 40 countries from 36 months to just 18 months."
- "It provides demonstrable corporate governance, improving business performance and pinpointing shortcomings costing more than £18m."
- "It has played a significant part in winning more than £30 million of new business and reducing costs by £5.7 million and projected annual savings of £4.5 million per annum."
- "We brought white-collar productivity up to match our envied blue-collar levels."

Crossing the Chasm and Inside the Tornado

By Geoffrey Moore published by Capstone

Moore's first book, *Crossing the Chasm* (1991), introduced readers to an updated view of the Technology Adoption Life Cycle, including a 'chasm' phase, which separates the early adopters from the mainstream market of pragmatic customers, and the strategies for making this market transition.

Inside the Tornado (1995) extends Moore's work with the Technology Adoption Life Cycle model to incorporate three distinct mainstream market stages: a pre-hypergrowth era of niche markets, the mass-market phenomenon of hypergrowth itself, and a post-hypergrowth era of mass customization. Moore illustrates the dynamics of each stage with examples from cutting-edge companies such as Hewlett-Packard, Microsoft, Intel, Sybase, PeopleSoft, and Lotus. He then goes on to analyze each stage's impact on strategic partnerships, competitive advantage, positioning, and organizational leadership.

Moore says, "The biggest challenge for management is that with each market phase transition, a new business strategy is called for – one that is not only different from their current strategy, but actually contradicts some of its core principles."

Inside the Tornado reaches out to companies beyond high-tech who are in technology-enabled or leveraged businesses, where the same market dynamics apply. This includes industries such as publishing and broadcasting, banking and finance, healthcare, as well as entertainment, where market forces are driving rapid re-engineering and new leaders are appearing overnight.

The critical success factor in each of these competitions, according to Moore, is to achieve "gorilla status" inside the tornado in order to be the market leader during the hypergrowth phase, which results in permanent advantages throughout the remainder of the life cycle. Timing is critical to this tornado strategy. Moore explains how to pool resources and gain supporters during the pre-tornado phase and then how to unleash them once the tornado hits. He also helps companies understand the post-tornado transition to a maturing market when companies must refocus on winning additional business from their installed base instead of seeking revenue growth from new customers.

The Empty Raincoat: Making Sense of the Future

By Charles Handy (1994), published by Random House Business Books

The book's theme is inspired by a statue in Minneapolis that provided the title: are we just 'empty raincoats' – units of labor and intellect – a cog in a corporate machine? Or is there someone of substance to fill the raincoat with meaning and purpose that goes beyond work?

"We were not destined to be empty raincoats, nameless numbers on a payroll, role occupants, the raw material of economics or sociology, statistics in some government report", he writes. "If that is to be its price, then economic progress is an empty promise." Handy believes that it is every individual's challenge to fill their empty raincoat.

To make meaning in their life.

It seems that success – both professional and economic – comes with a disproportionate cost attached, not necessarily for the wealthy few but certainly for the remainder of society. This is one of the greatest paradoxes of our time. Handy's book, *The Empty Raincoat*, addresses this issue along with other paradoxes that, he says, we must begin to face and manage.

Life, says Handy, is full of paradox. Not everything can be understood, predicted, or explained in full. One of the greatest paradoxes is the concept of choice. The freedom to choose for ourselves means that we have the ability to choose unwisely or wrongly. It is our challenge to manage the unavoidable paradoxes in our life, rather than strive for an impossible capitalist utopia based on individual material possessions.

Using colorful examples and analogies, the book offers a framework for the future of work and life in general. For organizations and individuals one of the first steps to change is the realization that business and personal security is not about land and buildings, but about knowledge.

The future will be owned by the workers because it will be based on their intelligence and know how – a difficult thing to gauge in financial terms alone. It will be like a 'virtual corporation' with a collection of permanent and temporary project groups existing more in a computer than in a set of shared offices. Work structures will be more about developing networks than honoring hierarchies and accepting responsibility not just blindly fulfilling core duties.

Handy uses a number of analogies to explain how these new structures could work:

The Sigmoid Curve illustrates that everything waxes and wanes: life, corporations, products, careers. It is critical to recognize where you are on the first S-curve plan to plan for the second before the first goes into decline. In today's fluid market that is more relevant now than ever.

The Doughnut Principle is a thought-provoking examination of work/life balance. With the finite amount of time you have represented by the outer circle, the amount of time you devote to work is the inner circle – how thick do you want your doughnut to be?

And the Chinese Contract is about the contracts we make with ourselves and others – are they equitable or are we being selfish?

The Art of the Start: The Time-Tested, Battle-Hardened Guide for Anyone Starting Anything

Guy Kawasaki (2004), published by Portfolio

When you get pregnant, you read What to Expect When you're Expecting. When you get laid off, you read *What Color is Your Parachute?* When you get entrepreneurial, you read *The Art of the Start.*

This book is a weapon of mass construction. The goal was to provide the definitive guide for anyone starting anything. It builds upon Kawasaki's experience as an evangelist, entrepreneur, and most recently, as a venture capitalist who found, fixed, and funded start-ups.

The book is as relevant for two guys in a garage starting the next Google as social activists trying to save the world. GIST (Great Ideas for Starting Things): cuts through the theoretical crap, theories and gets down to the real-world tactics of pitching, positioning, branding, recruiting, boot-strapping, and rainmaking.

The key entrepreneurial issues addressed in the book are:

- Positioning – Entrepreneurs must answer the critical questions of: why you want to start a business, why customers should patronize your business, and why good people should want to work for your business.
- Pitching – Successful entrepreneurs sell their ideas to others by getting a fast start, explaining their relevance, and staying out of the detail.
- Business Planning – Although very few people ever read an entire business plan, writing the business plan is still important as it forces a team to work together and formalize their intention. There are some components of the business plan that investors, recruits, and

potential Board members are really interested in and Kawasaki explains what should be included in these sections.

- Bootstrapping – One of an entrepreneur's real battles is surviving the critical, capital-deprived early days of any start-up's existence. According to Kawasaki, they need to pick the right business model, make cash king, and immediately get to market.

- Recruiting – Recruiting employees for a hot start-up is described as one of the most enjoyable tasks of an entrepreneur. In the process of recruiting, entrepreneurs should focus on three factors: (1) Can the candidate do what you need? (2) Does the candidate believe in the meaning that you are going to make? (3) Does the candidate have the strengths you need? (As opposed to the weaknesses you are trying to avoid.)

- Raising Capital – VCs want to know: Are you building something meaningful, long-lasting, and valuable to society? Kawasaki's experience in the VC industry empowers him to make some insightful and useful comments about what funders really look for in a business idea.

- Partnering – According to Kawasaki a good partnership should accelerate cash flow, increase revenue, and reduce costs. Partnerships must exist for valid business reasons.

- Branding – Branding a start-up is tough. Entrepreneurs need to focus on creating something that is contagious and infects people with enthusiasm. Branding is about community-building.

ARTICLE: LEADING VS. LAGGING METRICS

Are your managers operating as company doctors or coroners? A bizarre statement. Maybe, but are your executive management, managers, and supervisors using their business information delivered through reports and scorecards to "take the pulse of the organization" or "conduct a post mortem of last month's performance"?

Put another way. Are the Key Performance Indicators (KPIs) that they are using to make their decisions leading indicators or lagging indicators. Things can start to go wrong in a business well before the performance measure turns the traffic light on the scorecard red. Using metrics that measure past events is like driving while looking through the rear window.[72] You can easily miss the opportunity or threat on the road ahead until you're upon it.

Examples of lagging and leading indicators

So, if leading indicators are clearly more valuable than lagging, why do many (most) projects seem to deliver reports and scorecards full of lagging indicators? There are probably three reasons:

- Lagging numbers are the easiest to find in the corporate databases – they are the numbers that are found in the regular monthly reports.
- They are the easiest to identify, especially if you don't have intimate insights into the operation of the business (and many projects are given to IT to deliver).
- When IT are under pressure from the business to deliver "score-cards for the top team", they are the quickest way to satisfy the demand.

---

[72] Like most mothers driving monster 4 x 4's (SUVs) around the city filled with fighting kids.

LAGGING	LEADING
Software bugs reported to Support in Release x.x	Percentage of identified software bugs fixed in Release x.x
Q2 revenue	Contracts in negotiation for Q2
Call center calls completed within 2 minutes	Customer cases currently open
Product returns in November	Customer complaints, 3-month trend
Staff resignations in Q3	Increase in hits on www.monster.com in Q2, or Requests to HR for copies of employment contracts

So does it really matter? Well – yes

Firstly, delivering lagging indicators means that the business has a good idea of how well it has done, but little view of whether the direction/strategy is working. So not only is it wasting managers' time looking at reports which are only showing a historical position – but more importantly, it's squandering the opportunity to gain a competitive advantage. Remember, "if it's difficult for you, it's probably equally difficult for your competition".

Secondly, the promise or ROI from the scorecarding project is not being realized. Scorecards should not just be the latest management fad for senior management. They should be a valuable tool to aid decision-making in the hands of managers and supervisors – in fact, anyone managing a team. As this is clearly not happening, it's not surprising that Gartner in their famous 'Hype Cycle' see scorecarding as over the 'Peak of Inflated Expectations' and sliding down into the 'Trough of Disillusionment'.

Not a new problem

This is not a new problem. Just the terminology has changed, the technology is a little cheaper to implement, and the metrics easier to capture. Fifteen years ago, I was one of the IT Directors at the DSS, the UK Government Social Security organization. I had 500 staff in eight locations and a budget of £40m. In my rather large office (protected by a fierce secretary in her outer office), I had a PC with an executive information system (EIS) with lots of traffic lights reporting on my organization's performance.

I had no choice in setting the traffic lights or how the data that made them turn green, amber, or red was compiled. A complex application powered by mainframes crunched numbers for weeks to produce a set of traffic lights that only the Senior Directors saw. But those traffic lights weren't connected to any of our project processes or to any other definition of activity. I had no way of knowing what to do to change the traffic light from red to green. So I simply accepted the green lights and used the amber and red lights as early warnings to prepare my excuses for the next management meeting.

Having an EIS that creates performance data that isn't connected to an organization's activities is like trying to play a video game with a disconnected joystick. The game is still in play (people are still at work) but the joystick operator (management) can't influence the action.

Today's technology is better, so that data is produced more quickly and can come from more sources. But this doesn't make it any more useful at delivering a better result. If an improvement is needed to be able to catch up or hit a milestone, then my question was always the same "What are we going to do differently?" And "Work harder" is not necessarily the correct answer.

Changing the paradigm

To understand why projects are failing, we need to understand what is meant by failure:

- Scorecard projects are stalling and not being rolled out across the organization.
- The information on the scorecards is not supporting decision-making.

So how can we change the way we deliver scorecarding projects? We need to ensure that they help corporate decision-making at all levels in the organization, rather than having them become a senior executives' plaything. Like the 5-year-old with the new Xmas present – played with for a few weeks until the next new thing comes along – unless the scorecard adds real long-term value it will quickly be discarded, and never adopted at lower levels down the organization where it can do most good.

We need to change the idea that the scorecard is a collection of interesting numbers that people need to see, and think about it in a more structured way. There are two key principles which should be applied . . . 'top-down' and 'process-driven'.

Top-down and process-driven

Metrics are hierarchical, and therefore the metrics which are driving the behaviors of junior supervisors, managers, and executives should all be in alignment. That means the overall KPIs of the business should be identified first – which they normally are. You can often spot some of them in the company's Annual Reports. The difficulty is then breaking these down to lower levels, which is where the second principle comes in: 'process-driven'.

Unless you have a clear understanding at every level of the organization what the end-to-end process is, then it's very difficult to identify the correct metrics to drive the business. Remember – you get what you measure, so measure the wrong thing and you get the wrong behaviors.

You may be able to identify the metrics at the highest level or even the second or third level, but at the lowest levels it becomes impossible to identify metrics which are "leading AND aligned with the goals of the organization". To achieve both these objectives you will need to develop the process and metrics hierarchy in parallel – each feeding the other.

Putting it into practice

At the highest level there are five or six key activities, each of which has a metric. So for example, for a credit card company, the top-level process and related metrics – driven out of a live workshop with the top team – may look like in Figure 13.

Each activity can be broken down into lower and lower levels of detail, each with the same simple diagramming structure of 'input–activity–output', and from that the leading and lagging indicators at each level will (surprisingly) pop out fairly quickly.

This combines the principles of Balanced Scorecard and the process improvement techniques such as LEAN or Six Sigma. The benefits of this dual approach are:

- Alignment of the end-to-end processes from the senior management level down to the 'shop floor'.
- Alignment of the metrics senior management level down to the 'shop floor'.
- Leading indicators identified at each level.

The final word – agility

Think about driving alongside a pavement crowded with Christmas shoppers. A pedestrian steps out and, thanks to your lightning reactions and the ABS on your car, you manage to avoid hitting them. So, agility is whether you are able to respond if something jumps out in front of you. The measure is "did you hit them?" You could have been just as 'agile', but required a far less violent reaction if you had been alert to the possibility and had earlier warning of the pedestrian's actions.

There is a strong parallel with corporations. Many are striving to be so nimble that they can change direction in an instant, but are failing because a nimble 10,000-person organization is an oxymoron. It's

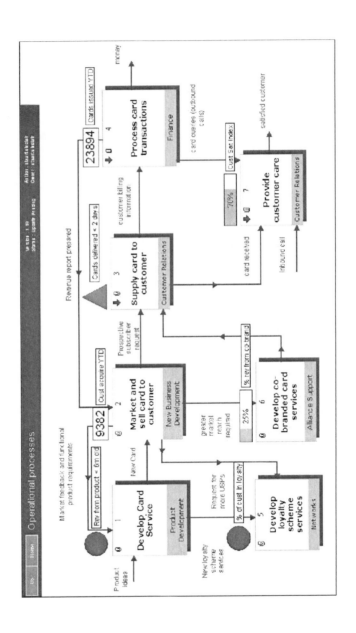

impossible, especially when you realize the increasing demands to comply with various legislation. So, surely a better approach is to be prepared for change (process) and have early warning (leading metrics).

ARTICLE: RUNNING SENIOR MANAGEMENT WORKSHOPS

The OCA methodology takes you through mapping the current operation, and then mapping the operations which correspond to the buying cultures you need to support. It recommends that you use workshops to drive out a shared view of the operation.

My experience is that process mapping in live workshops is infinitely quicker, more productive, and drives genuine adoption. The alternative approach is interviewing people, and this is normally an expensive, time-wasting disaster.

Therefore, I prepared the approach to running senior-level workshops as a series of checklists:

Preparation

- Company mission/vision/strategy from Chairman's Report in Annual Report or website
- Scope of project from project proposal and scope document
- Objective of workshop from project sponsor or project manager
- Personal objectives of CEO, project sponsor, and project manager
- Scope and context of workshop
- Audience – name, role, title
- What personal conflicts and politics in the group, and where is power
- Terminology – what will turn them on, turn them off, no-no's

- How much understanding and buy-in does the audience have of buying cultures, operational cultures, and processes
- What is the pain to resolve
- Where is ROI or win
- Get Non-Disclosure Agreement (NDA) signed by third-party facilitator

Agenda/sequence

- Introductions – go around the room
- Introduce session – why they are there, pain, ...
- Objectives of the session – working meeting to get a result
- Benefits of session –
  - defines company operational strategy
  - sets context for specific projects
  - sets priorities for improvement projects
  - kick start projects
  - identifies project sponsors and demonstrates support
- Show 'finished product' – so they know what they are aiming at (include showing them the attachments and measures)
- Strategic objectives on white board (tangible – with measures)
- Mapping from end point back
- Identify priority processes for initial projects
- Next steps

Conducting the process mapping

- The most important thing is to get interaction and momentum – get them talking/arguing
- Start with blank sheet
- Start at back end of process "bill and collect payment" because it's easy, non-contentious, and it gets the ball rolling

- Then move forward "what allows you to create the invoice"
- Don't worry about inputs and outputs initially, but as the debate grows between audience about the context and scope of each activity use the input and output to define
- Use the notes bubbles to document what the lower-level activities are (if and when they get talked about) – try to avoid drilling down as it distracts from the top level
- To get them to focus on activities use "I have just joined your organization as a XXXX, and I need to XXX. How do I know what to do next? How do I know when I've finished"
- If they can't agree, move to a whiteboard to sketch a flow of processes, then go back and map

Handling issues and objections

- Can't agree on certain activities
  - revert to whiteboard
  - try to define inputs and outputs
  - look to CEO/sponsor to resolve
- Don't have the correct people in the room
  - check if workshop results will be considered 'agreed'
  - look to CEO/sponsor to resolve
- People focus on departments or reporting lines not processes
  - ask the "I do XXXX, how can I understand what to do?" questions
- IT-focused people describe in systems (automated process) terms rather than the complete process
  - ask the "I do XXXX, how can I understand what to do?" questions